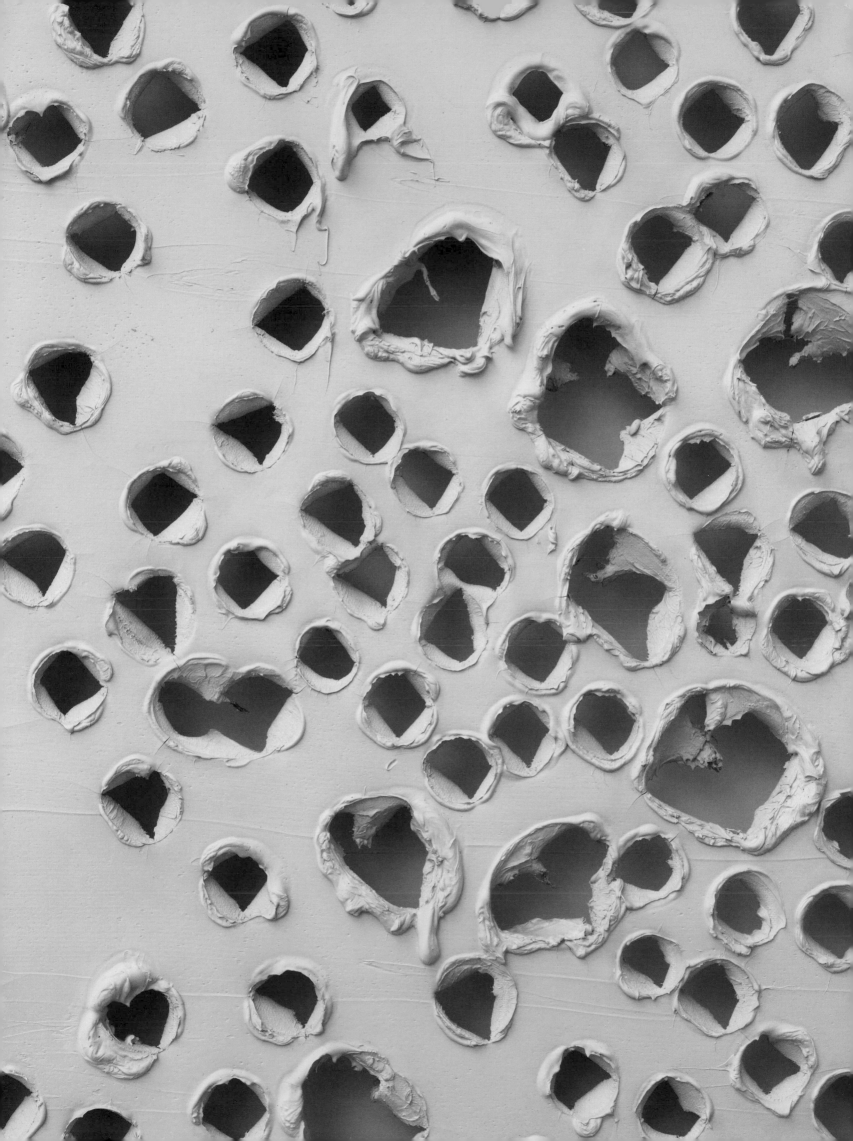

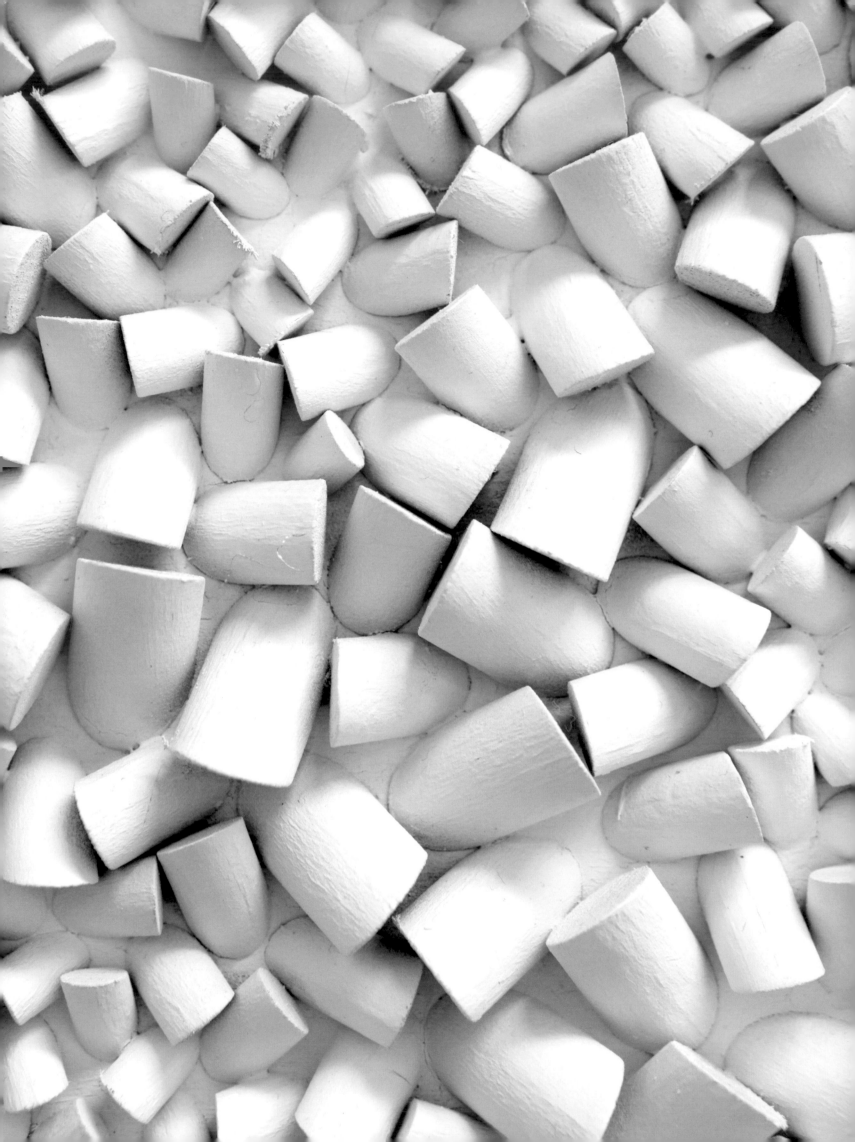

For Vernon Faulconer (1939–2015)

AETRIES

ON AND OFF THE GRID

GEOM

ART FROM 1950 TO THE PRESENT

CURATED BY

ALLAN SCHWARTZMAN

The Warehouse

CONTENTS

PREFACE AND ACKNOWLEDGMENTS

Vernon Faulconer and I initiated The Warehouse project to make our collections available to curators, scholars, critics, and students and to open new dialogues about postwar modern and contemporary art. At the heart of the project is an adapted industrial building in Dallas, containing art storage facilities, an extensive library, and eighteen thousand square feet of flexible exhibition space. Here, The Warehouse presents carefully considered, original exhibitions of works from our own collections, complemented by art acquired jointly with the Dallas Museum of Art (DMA) and works on loan from other significant institutions and private collections. These changing exhibitions are developed specifically to suggest new perspectives on art and to invite fresh questions that expand accepted notions of history. We place our collections at the service of the artistic community in the hope that they may be used as a resource for research and learning and to create new ideas that may be shared with a broad audience.

Geometries On and Off the Grid: Art from 1950 to the Present examines geometry in the art of the postwar period and endeavors to posit a global view that is more wide ranging than the perspective from which this history has generally been traced in collections, exhibitions, and scholarship. One hundred and twelve artists from eighteen countries are represented here. Much of the material may be unfamiliar and that which is not is presented in what we hope will be found as inventive combinations that inform and reorient our understanding of this crucial period in art history.

This exhibition is at core a collaboration between our dear friends Marguerite Steed Hoffman, Deedie Rose, and Sharon and Michael Young, with whom it is our pleasure and privilege to partner both in collecting and in attempting to build a cultural legacy for our city. We are ever thankful to them and to the DMA for lending to the exhibition and for so generously parting with works from their collections for this important endeavor. Much of the art here has been acquired with or given as gifts, fully or in part, to the DMA; in time, virtually all of it will belong to the museum. May this exhibition serve as a rough draft for the museum and provide a unique perch from which the institution may inform its priorities for building its own collection and exhibitions. It has always been our belief that these collaborative ambitions position Dallas to be a leader in the visual arts. We are proud that through the range and depth of geometric art represented here, Dallas is contributing to the international rethinking of art in the postwar period that is currently developing in museum and scholarly communities around the world. To realize *Geometries On and Off the Grid*, many individuals came together offering support.

The conception and realization of an exhibition and publication like this would not have been possible without the care and commitment of Allan Schwartzman. His enthusiasm for the work of postwar artists has been this project's touchstone. With his enduring vision, he has organized another influential exhibition that allows The Warehouse to accomplish its educational mission.

The Warehouse staff claims a significant share in realizing this project, and we are deeply appreciative of their goodwill. We owe special thanks to Meg Smith Gratch, Manager of Curatorial Projects, Thomas Feulmer, Director of Educational Programming, Caitlin Overton, Gallery Teacher, Jeanne Chvosta, Collections Manager, Sara Deal, Assistant Registrar, Jodie Oliver, Events Director, and Abel Hernandez and Tony Silva, all of whom were crucial to and supportive of this endeavor.

We are also indebted to a superior team of professionals: Gavin Delahunty, Hoffman Family Senior Curator of Contemporary Art at the Dallas Museum of Art, who contributed a moving essay; David Zaza and Michelle Lee Nix at McCall Associates, who designed the book; Frances Bowles, who edited the text; the photographer Kevin Todora, who documented the works and installations; and Anna Kern, the bibliographer. We value each of these colleagues greatly for their support, dedication, and expertise and are deeply grateful to them for helping us realize this exhibition and publication.

Finally, we offer our respect, admiration, and heartfelt appreciation to the artists who made this exhibition a reality. It is with tremendous enthusiasm that The Warehouse brings their important contributions to the attention of the wider public.

Ordinarily, Vern would have written this preface with me. Tragically, and unexpectedly, he passed away just as we began writing these words. The Warehouse, the exhibition, and this catalogue are a fulfillment of the spirit of curiosity, generosity, and sharing that were at the core of Vern's humble, caring being. We dedicate this book to him.

HOWARD RACHOFSKY

INTRODUCTION

Three families—the Hoffmans, Rachofskys, and Roses—each, in its own way, passionate about collecting contemporary art—came together as dear friends and "co-conspirators" to support a notion about art and community that was bigger than they themselves, in hopes of creating something lasting and accessible for their city and its citizens. Together, they decided to donate their collections to the Dallas Museum of Art, and that declaration of common commitment has informed their collecting—individually and collaboratively—ever since. This exhibition, *Geometries On and Off the Grid: Art from 1950 to the Present*, had its genesis in discussions over dinners and art journeys to Venice, Basel, and Napa, California, occasions that prompted conversations about the various ways in which it would be possible to create a critical mass of appreciation for and understanding of contemporary art by merging these individual collections with the great holdings of the Dallas Museum of Art.

The specific idea of looking at the language of geometry in the postwar period coalesced as a response to *Fast Forward: Contemporary Collections for the Dallas Museum of Art*, an exhibition organized by María de Corral at the Dallas Museum of Art in 2006. That exhibition offered the first glimpse of what this future legacy could look like. Recognizing in it not only a great wealth of postwar geometric abstraction but also what might distinguish Dallas's holdings from those of other museums in this country and elsewhere, the collectors and I began to envision the show documented in this present catalogue. Since then, the development of the collections has been driven by the commitment to contribute to the wealth of art in Dallas and to encourage fresh thinking about our understanding of art from the postwar period through to the present.

ALLAN SCHWARTZMAN
Exhibition Curator and Director of the Rachofsky and Rose Collections

CONTINGENT GEOMETRIES

GAVIN DELAHUNTY

Modernism is a complex of interlocking dimensions, its relations deriving their meaning from their dialectical interplay with one another. Beginning with the parsimonious arrangements and industrial materials of Minimalism, this exhibition, *Geometries On and Off the Grid: Art from 1950 to the Present*, goes on to destabilize this mode of abstraction by introducing work that is organic, dynamic, or in flux. Moreover, as one moves through the exhibition, it becomes clear that the New York art world conjured by the first gallery is radically decentered. Art from the 1950s onward departs from established art historical narratives to be replaced by a situation that is characterized by pluralism and by the absence of any dominant style, geographic center, or philosophy—a single, hegemonic voice has been supplanted by a cacophony of voices vying for our attention. Sometimes, in uncovering concrete dialogues or lines of influence, the works in this exhibition, from North America, Europe, Latin America, and Asia, make more speculative and precarious connections that ignite new ways of thinking. In this essay, the strategies of liminality, dialecticism, hybridity, corporeality, and virality, which have eroded the autonomy of the modernist art object, are considered in the light of key works from the exhibition.

LIMINALITY

By the grace of god I grew up in that beautiful place [Easton, Maryland] . . . that beautiful peninsula. Very flat land, where the water and land are virtually exchangeable, interchangeable, in some cases barely discernable one from the other.
—Anne Truitt[1]

Four monumental black canvases painted by Frank Stella and exhibited at the Museum of Modern Art, New York, in 1959 as part of the exhibition *16 Americans* initiated a period during which the boundaries of painting and sculpture began to be crossed (fig. 1). Because they were rejecting pictorial illusion, painters such as Stella started taking into account issues of three-dimensional work, while sculptors such as Anne Truitt began to deal with issues of color that had previously been confined to painting. Take Stella's *Valparaiso Green*, 1963 (pp. 38–39) for example. With its unprecedented depth, shaped support, and absence of a frame, it confronts you, as much a physical object as it is a vehicle for color. *Valparaiso Green* is composed of three triangles, each made up of fourteen chevron patterns. The V-shaped arrangement in the central section is upright, with the flanking sections both facing downward. There is a symmetry to the work. Standing in front of the painting, one has the impression of weight—perhaps a result of Stella's use of metallic paint. The monochromatic palette, in this instance green, adds to the sense of equilibrium, unifying at the same time as it articulates. Stella explained: "A symmetrical image or configuration placed on an open ground is not balanced out in illusionistic space. The solution

I arrived at . . . color density—forces illusionistic space out of the painting at a constant rate by using regulated pattern."[2] Although the work is composed of rigid geometric forms, there is a peculiar flow to it as the repeated stripes direct the eye to each of its four corners. By eliminating all attributes not consistent with the flat surface and the two dimensionality, the artist increases the feeling of painting as object and, in doing so, expands the formal possibilities of painting.

Sculptors working in the 1960s such as Donald Judd, Anne Truitt, and Charlotte Posenenske moved away from materials and techniques previously associated with the medium, to give the illusion of something autonomous and new, without reference to history. Their use of color, found or painted, enables their objects to appear lighter or heavier and maximizes their ability to assert themselves in an environment. Truitt's *Valley Forge*, 1963 (p. 40 and detail, p. 23) has a brush-worked surface that found its equivalents in a type of mark making prevalent in painting during the 1960s. In a review of Truitt's exhibition at the André Emmerich Gallery in 1963 (fig. 2), Michael Fried commented that "the relation of Miss Truitt's fine, intelligent work to that of painters [Ellsworth] Kelly [fig. 3], [Ray] Parker and [Ad] Reinhardt is unmissable." He avoided mentioning any sculptural counterparts. A solid rectangle in deep ruby red and crimson,

Fig. 1. Frank Stella, *Black Paintings*, installation view of the exhibition *16 Americans*, the Museum of Modern Art, New York, December 16, 1959– February 16, 1960

Fig. 2. Anne Truitt's sculpture, installation view of the exhibition *Truitt: First New York Exhibition*, the André Emmerich Gallery, New York, February 12–March 3, 1963

Fig. 3. Ellsworth Kelly, *Red, Yellow, Blue*,
1963. Fondation Marguerite et Aimé
Maeght, Saint-Paul, France

Truitt's sculpture is raised off the floor, appearing weightless. Three-fifths of the surface of the sculpture are given over to three horizontal bands—two thinner bands at the top and bottom and one significantly wider central band. The other two-fifths are oriented vertically and share an equal amount of space. One of the vertical sections is detailed by a semicircular groove on the surface. The gouge isolates and draws our attention to this section. When one follows the groove by eye, the hand-painted quality of the sculpture becomes apparent, with a number of the painted lines breaching the ostensibly rigid geometric construction. A technique of very dense cross-hatching seems to have been used, finished with a layer of close, linear hatching. Like Stella, who took advantage of the paint bleeding and soaking into the raw, untreated canvas in his paintings, Truitt considered the absorbency of wood a key feature and stressed that it was instrumental in unifying color and material. Reflecting her broader interest in thresholds and meeting points, such as the shoreline between land and sea, Truitt's work exists in a liminal space between painting and sculpture.

DIALECTICISM

My work has always been an attempt to get away from the specific object. My objects are constantly moving into another area . . . they are things rather than definable presences.
—Robert Smithson[3]

Robert Smithson radically deconstructed the sculptural object by bringing unconventional materials from the natural world into the gallery, to create a dialectical relationship between that institutional space and a place or occurrence in the outside world. He thereby called into question the display of artwork in this gallery, as opposed to external objects, things, and sites. Smithson was interested in triggering instability in what we perceive to be a designation of place. The beginning and end of *Mirrors and Shelly Sand*, 1969–70 (pp. 72–73) are determined by the entryway into the room in which the work is installed. At a certain distance the work appears to be a solid green rectangular box, which is set on a bed of sand and on which a triangular prism of sand is resting. Up close, however, the cuboid is seen as twenty-five identical horizontal sheets of mirror, each propped up by minute fragments of shells. The distinctive green tint that was seen from a distance is caused by iron, which is an impurity in the sand that was used to make the mirrored glass. Each sheet consists of two mirrors, assembled back-to-back, that are roughly one foot tall and evenly spaced from the next set by approximately one foot. The mirrors are partially buried in the shell sand. The hill-like profiles of the sand on either side of each of the mirror inserts start low, at each end of the rectangular mirror, where the mirror has transected the sand, and rise almost to the top of the glass in the middle. This type of sand has been created over the past half billion years by various forms of life, such as coral and shellfish. Paradoxically, the shelly sand is, on a molecular level, intricately structured while the mirrors—being amorphous solids, and which appear in precise strata—have no crystalline structure.

The first mirror facing outward reflects the sand piled in front and the floor of the room in which it is installed. The reverse side faces the second mirror, creating a reflective chamber. These mirrors can reflect only the contents of the space between them. The interaction between panes two and three is repeated between panes four and five, six and seven, eight and nine, and so on, up to panes forty-eight and forty-nine. The reflection of the last pane, number fifty, is the reverse of that of the first one: the sand piled behind it and, again, the floor of the room. Because the mirrors are reflecting the same shelly sand, they convey an illusion of transparency, as if they were clear glass. A further illusion appears as you make your way around the sculpture. The tops of the sandwiched pairs create an impression of dark lines hovering above the sand. As you circumnavigate the work, the lines appear and disappear depending on where you are.

Like Smithson, Richard Serra exposes the elemental material properties of his chosen medium but only to stress its intrinsic sculptural potential and those issues and procedures that are essential to the execution of the specific work. *Close Pin Prop*, 1969–76 (p. 71 and detail, p. 55), is composed of two tightly rolled columns of lead. One column is held perpendicular to the wall by the weight of the other column, which is propped against it but not fixed in any way. In an arrangement Serra described as "stitching," he puts to use the very first means of raising forms from the ground, such as leaning and propping, that a child might use. Whereas the drama in Smithson's work lies in his ability to simulate an imaginary encounter between the viewer and a distant site, the anxiety in Serra's work is generated by the dialectical tension between the two components and their physical proximity to the viewer.

While Serra and Smithson investigated the rational interaction between and with specific materials, Nobuo Sekine applied materials to produce optical illusions or create perceptual tricks. Sekine's experiments with trompe l'œil devices exploited the rational relationship of things such as canvas, rope, stone, wood, and water in a way that imbued them with eye-catching illusionism.[4] The center of Sekine's white canvas *Phase of Nothingness—Cloth and Stone*, 1970/1994 (p. 74 and detail, p. vii), has been gathered into a small bunch, shaped like a ball, that is held in position by an anchor knot from which a long piece of rope is suspended. The other end of the rope is fastened around a large stone—the mass of the stone forcing the canvas to pleat. The energy Serra uses to arrange his materials in a stabilized position obeys basic physics as they relate to mass and gravity. In contrast, Sekine's work overturns the laws of balance. However, it also creates tension for the viewer. One might expect that the vertical downward pull on the fabric by the weight of the stone would, in normal circumstances, cause a tear in the canvas. This expectation triggers an anxiety that strikes right at the heart of the concept of the work of art as a physical object designed for posterity. In that sense Sekine's work could be described as anti-art, its illusionism subverting received definitions about the role and function of art.

HYBRIDITY

I am not here representing Brazil, or anything else; the ideas of representing, representation, are over.
—Hélio Oiticica[5]

Earlier generations of Brazilian artists had certainly rejected pictorial representation, but Hélio Oiticica's catalogue entry for the Museum of Modern Art's exhibition *Information*, in 1970, criticized the curatorial representation of race, ethnicity, and gender in large-scale surveys of contemporary art (fig. 4). Oiticica was not content to be solely a representative of Brazil. He saw himself as a hybrid of modernity. In his legendary statement Oiticica seemed to be challenging the very idea of culture—understood as a set of common beliefs that hold people together—and Western hegemony in relation to the visual arts. In his view, stereotypical notions of identity and cultural singularity were ripe for infiltration and growth. It was an appeal that shaped subsequent attitudes toward exhibition making, prompting artists, critics, and curators to explore the richness and diversity of postwar art and to create hybridizations and new meanings.

Oiticica's *Untitled*, 1970 (pp. 162–63), brings together color, space, light, and movement as formal instruments. A wooden spatial relief in four shades of yellow is suspended from the ceiling. The central shape is a hexagon composed of a square and two congruent isosceles triangles. The other two parts are also hexagons, each composed of a square and two triangles with an area and perimeter equal to the middle section. Before being added to the right- and left-hand sides of the central hexagon, the outer two hexagons have had their triangles positioned at different obtuse angles, creating a space-filling shape with two enclosed structures. The four shades of yellow draw our attention to new shapes that have been created both inside and outside the two chambers. The structure was inspired by the makeshift houses in Brazil's favelas and was suspended so that it could be navigated bodily and experienced with all the senses. Along with other artists of the neo-Concrete movement, such as Lygia

Clark and Mira Schendel, Oiticica deconstructed the disciplines of the formal language of geometric abstraction in order to produce hybrid, contingent works that "express complex human realities."[6]

Schendel's *Untitled*, 1963 (p. 104), is composed of four units, two smaller ones set in front of two larger rectangles, one of which is painted in a coffee color, the other, chocolate. The two smaller elements in the foreground are divided by a more or less untouched part of the canvas. These elements are lifted from their dry, matte background by a thick application of paint. In particular the compositional element on the right, the lighter and more intense of the two, appears to have been built up using short strokes necessitated by the fast-drying, glutinous tempera paint used. The result is a section that has a sculptural quality to its surface and seems to have been composed in plaster or painted wood. The question of that dual character—the relation between painting and sculpture, picture and object—is also dealt with in Yves Klein's *Untitled Monogold*, 1961 (p. 101). Klein's monochromes could be seen as objects, their literal presence enhanced by the process of their making—here the gold material beaten onto the plywood substrate. As pictures, they approached a condition of objecthood akin to sculpture or the pictorial quality of a three-dimensional object that has been hammered out from some malleable, ductile metal. Overall there is a strong organic, natural feel to Klein's and Schendel's work that is the result of their truth to materials and pure form, which in itself conveys a certain beauty. This is extended in a more explicitly biomorphic direction in the work of Schendel's contemporary Lygia Clark.

Clark's interactive work *Bicho—Em si* (*Creature—In Itself*), 1962 (p. 153), is a hinged metal object made from a series of connected geometric planes. Viewers are invited to move it into various configurations. In the act of manipulation, the viewer is breathing life into the ostensibly lifeless aluminum object (fig. 5). "It demands of the spectator an integral participation, a will to knowledge and participation."[7] Clark intended the viewer to regard the *bichos* as living organisms: "the interlinking of the spectators' action and the 'animals' is what forms this new relationship, made possible precisely because the 'animal' moves—i.e., has a life of its own."[8] With meaning left ambiguous, emphasis is instead placed on the marriage between the functionality of the object and the operator's fingers. Rather than signaling a retreat from worldly concerns, the formal elegance of the *bicho* invites the spectator's direct, tactile engagement. Combining art and therapy, sculpture and performance, Clark's work embraces hybridity and contingency.

Fig. 4. Installation view of the exhibition *Information*, the Museum of Modern Art, New York, July 2–September 20, 1970

Fig. 5. Lygia Clark manipulating *Bicho* (*Creature*), 1960

CORPOREALITY

Now I wasn't just making shapes to look at; by saying "these are templates of my body,"
I gave them reason enough for their existence.
—Bruce Nauman[9]

Ideas about the body and how those might merge with minimal tendencies in art were of critical importance in the mid-1960s. A number of artists were as interested in referencing the body as they were in the processes by which an art object is made. Certain artists working in North America during this period can be compared to adherents of the neo-Concrete movement in the sense that their work was also conditioned by the changing social aspirations of the 1960s. They were highly educated, empowered, and called for political, intellectual, and artistic freedom. The language of the body constituted a response to the social, political, sexual, and cultural upheavals of the time. Artists such as Bruce Nauman and Hannah Wilke developed viable mutations of Minimalism when it was at the height of its dominance in America.

Nauman rejected the strict geometry and symmetry that characterized classic Minimalism. On the whole, he crafted his works by hand rather than having them manufactured by an outside fabricator. *Untitled*, 1965 (p. 259), a long, slender, irregular shape, is a cast fiberglass sculpture of the outer part of his own shoulder, elbow, wrist, knee, and ankle. The fiberglass and polyester resin make the work look, to some degree, aged. The surface resembles skin, the effect of whatever textile material was used to protect his skin before the synthetic materials were applied to his body to form the shape. Patchwork layers of this fabric are still visible as are their gridded weaves, fraying at the edges where they have been cut into strips for application. Furthermore, the entire surface of the cast is cracked as if to suggest some trauma or infection. The sense of infection is intensified by the pale greenish-yellow color. Where the plastic and resin have dried, fissures have erupted and extend the length of the work. The work is an abstraction, in the sense of capturing or seizing a fragment of the imperceptible line that contours the body.

The relationship of this sculpture to the body is not only acknowledged by the artist but also is implicit in a performance piece that Nauman executed while studying at the University of California at Davis in 1965 (fig. 6). For that performance he assumed consecutive poses (standing, leaning, bending, squatting, sitting, and lying down), each held for a minute, while positioned in one of four varying stances relative to a wall: facing the wall, with his back to the wall, and then facing either ninety degrees to the left or to the right. Shortly thereafter, he began casting the body in works such as the present *Untitled*. Referring to this work of Nauman's in the mid-1960s, Robert Pincus-Witten observed that, "in many respects these 'impoverished'

Figs. 6 a–f. Bruce Nauman, images from *Wall-Floor Positions*, 1968. Videotape, black and white, sound, 60 minutes

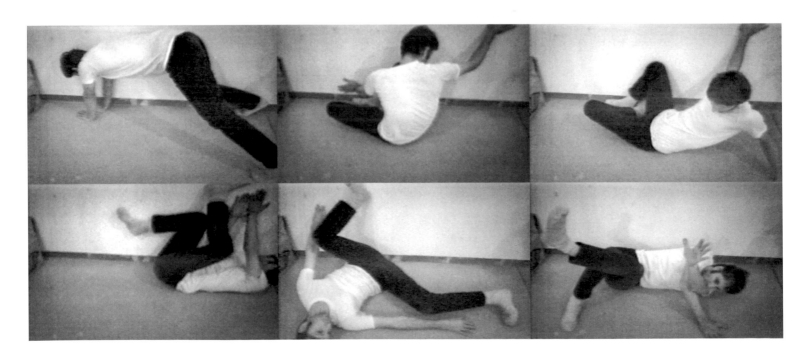

works, supported directly by the wall and floor, anticipate many of the experiments associated with the rise of post-Minimalism—particularly the early rubber and neon works of Richard Serra."[10] But, while Serra's sculpture, and much of post-Minimalism, tended toward abstraction, Nauman's work figures the human body.

Nauman was included in Lucy Lippard's groundbreaking exhibition *Eccentric Abstraction* (1966, fig. 7), along with important women artists, among them Alice Adams, Louise Bourgeois, and Eva Hesse. Although concerned with the body, the exhibition and its catalogue eschewed the politics of gender. What it did was to invite assessment and reassessment by key critics at that time who were investigating creativity through the lens of the Feminist Art Movement. "When I first heard . . . about the high incidence of central core-imagery, of boxes, ovals, spheres, and 'empty' containers, in women's art, I vehemently resisted [the inference]," Lippard wrote.[11] Yet ten years after *Eccentric Abstraction*, she acknowledged that traits associated with women's understanding of themselves were undeniably present in the work of several women artists connected with post-Minimalism: "a uniform density, or overall texture, often sensuously tactile and repetitive or detailed to the point of obsession . . . a certain kind of fragmentation; a new fondness of the pinks and pastels and ephemeral cloud colors that used to be taboo unless a woman wanted to be accused of making 'feminine' art."[12] Lippard's statement became a key account of the presence and importance of a new artistic language of body-centered woman-hood in the work of artists including Hannah Wilke.

Wilke, like Nauman, set herself apart through her ingenious use of color. "From 1960 to 1963 I worked in ceramics, creating layered vaginal forms in natural browns and terracotta. I added color in around 1963, pink ceramics, and that's when the vulvic forms evolved."[13] *Untitled*, 1975–78 (p. 243 and detail, p. 10) consists of sixty, small, colored ceramic sculptures that have a consistent form suggestive of a vagina, labia, or urethra. Their arrangement on a low wooden platform for display follows a certain set of orderly rows although they do not adhere to it entirely. Simple, sensuous, and subtle in their variation, these innovative sculptural forms move beyond the bodily suggestiveness of Nauman and, in doing so, make a claim for explicit expressions of female sexual experience. Genital imagery is thus located within a lineage of conceptual self-confidence and formal invention.

Rachel Whiteread's *Untitled (Air Bed)*, 1992 (p. 293), is a further adjustment of the way in which artists might reference the body in the objects that they make. One of the

Fig. 7. Installation view of the exhibition *Eccentric Abstraction*, **the Fishbach Gallery, New York, 1966**

characteristics of Whiteread's work is that it, too, falls between abstraction and figuration. It is abstract in the sense of its incorporeal dimension—what the artist often casts has no material existence, these are ghost spaces. They include the interior spaces of a house or the areas between bookshelves and beneath chairs and staircases. It is figurative in the sense that her subjects are domestic objects that we inhabit or furniture or constructions that we use and which signify some trace of their users. Her work generates ideas of visibility and hiddenness. *Untitled (Air Bed)* is a cast of an inflated air bed that has been placed directly on the floor. The surface has an uneven texture that is imprinted by the casting technique with the familiar contours, albeit in reverse, of an air mattress. Despite the obvious care taken in casting, there is an abundance of imprecisions that distinguish the cast from its referent—you certainly would not want to sleep on this undulating mattress. Where the casting material made its way into the crevasses of the PVC form, noticeable sharp peaks have been created that look as if they would jab and possibly injure. Her casts are not a surrogate for an absent object; although they do depend on other objects, they are in effect a facsimile of absence. This could be taken even a step further, with the notion that the works demonstrate the impossibility of representation.

VIRALITY

I want to be like a virus that belongs to the institution. If I function like a virus, an imposter, an infiltrator, I will always replicate myself together with those institutions.
—Félix González-Torres[14]

In a move of aesthetic liberation, Félix González-Torres took the vocabulary of the 1960s and radicalized it with intensely private experiences of vulnerability, ephemerality, and loss. *"Untitled"* (*7 Days of Bloodworks*), 1988 (p. 287 and detail, p. 278), consists of seven white canvases with fine graphite lines that make up a regular grid. The grids call to mind graph paper, which is often used as a guide for plotting particular information—a means to measure the ascent and descent of certain figures. On each canvas, the grid is intersected by a single diagonal line, which starts and finishes at a consistent point on the graph. In some of the canvases, the grid is barely discernable and only the diagonal line is observable; in others, the diagonal line is hardly detectable and only the grid is obvious. The title, *"Untitled"* (*7 Days of Bloodworks*), implies a hematology test, part of a general investigation of an acute illness. The underlying sense from the work— each cell of the graph corresponding to the cell count of the patient—is that there is some deficiency or weakening taking place. Whether the sloping line is rising or falling is not made explicit, but the overall white gesso color appears to be suppressing a red hue that is concealed deep within the canvas. The repetition of the results across seven canvases certainly alludes to impending defeat, the overpowering use of white suffocating and the clinical-looking line describing a worrying outcome.

A number of works that refer to medical processes were made over six years. In 1989 the artist used graphite, colored pencil, and tempera on paper and arranged the works in two and five parts. In 1990 he made versions, called *"Untitled"* (*T-Cell Count*), using graphite, colored pencil, and gouache, on single sheets of paper. The works make explicit the relationship between this series and the Acquired Immune Deficiency Syndrome (AIDS), which causes inefficiencies in T-cell function, T-cells being a type of white blood cell that plays a central role in defense against disease. In 1991 *"Untitled"* (*31 Days of Bloodworks*), the largest work from the series, develops from the earlier week of bloodwork to a month of bloodwork. In 1992 *"Untitled"* (*False Hope—Bloodwork*) appears, followed by *"Untitled"* (*Bloodwork—Steady Decline*) in 1993, that year concluding with the devastating *"Untitled"* (*9 Days of Bloodwork—Steady Decline and False Hope*). Four more versions appear in 1994 but with titles that relapse to earlier versions: *"Untitled"* (*19 Days of Bloodwork—Steady Decline*), *"Untitled"* (*21 Days of Bloodwork—Steady Decline*), and *"Untitled"* (*Bloodwork—Steady Decline*). The artist died of AIDS in Miami in 1996, and these works, some of the last he ever made, serve to emphasize the deterioration.

González-Torres, like almost no other contemporary artist, was aware of his own past, present, and future. "The nature of his work in general . . . subtly yet emphatically intensifies one's own self-awareness, subjectivity, and sense of personal history. In effect, his work insists upon the inclusion of the complexities of those areas most preciously protected or deeply repressed—it sets up a conflation of public and private, and the personal with the professional."[15]

Mark Bradford's *A Truly Rich Man is One Whose Children Run Into His Arms When His Hands are Empty*, 2008 (pp. 328–29 and detail, p. 310), instantly evokes a snapshot taken from an airplane roughly thirty-seven thousand feet above a modern city at night and capturing that otherworldly, aerial view we are all familiar with. Bradford's work is very much of the earth-bound world, its powerful networks and economies. He states: "People post up signs advertising everyday trades. These people know exactly who will see the signs. Signs for divorce, electrical, and hair braiding services explode down the boulevard. On fences there is an additive and subtractive relationship that I translate somehow into my practice."[16] The focus of Bradford's project is addressed in this comment, with his consciousness of labor, audience, and the relentlessly evolving stage for production and presentation. This work also calls to mind ideas of surveillance—although Bradford knows that an examination of a metropolitan area simply in terms of its built topography is increasingly inadequate in a digital era. Put simply, topographical information is well suited for representing travel between points and illustrating the shortest paths through a network, but it does not map digital networks. Recently a layer has emerged as a means of communicating, connecting people within a network of networks, fiber-optic cables that supply telecommunications to large sections of society. "When we talk about the Internet, we talk about clouds and ether. But the Internet is not amorphous. You may access it wirelessly, but ultimately you are relying on a bunch of physical cables."[17] This expansive network of cables enables images, videos, and pieces of information to spread rapidly from one Internet user to another, in a manner we now describe as viral.

Bradford's process of collage and décollage starts with a collection of paper materials found in his neighborhood. These he overlaps in successive layers before subjecting the entire surface to a series of abrasive abstractions such as scraping, sanding, grinding, and scouring that eliminate almost all traces of the original sources. Like the thoroughfares and junctures that carry Internet traffic, any imagery in his work remains elusive. "The tacit argument that his subjects are unpresentable issues from Bradford's commitment to the informal economies that interest him, which operate off the grid, in the shadows, eschewing a public face and a public voice for the sake of subsistence."[18] Bradford resists straightforward representation while infusing an abstract vocabulary with social and political meaning.

In the abstract art of the early twentieth century, the use of geometrical structures often signaled a retreat from representation into an ideal space divorced from the world outside. This autonomous sphere—central to the concept of modernism—came under attack in the second half of the century, when artists began to invest forms such as the polygon, the polyhedron, and the grid with somatic, psychological, ecological, and political connotations. Without reverting to mimetic forms of representation, artists as diverse as Truitt, Sekine, Oiticica, and Whiteread have used geometrical structures that are contingent upon and suggestive of the world at large. Stella once insisted that his paintings be taken at face value—stating that "what you see is what you see."[19] Bradford treats painting as a densely layered field, loaded with references to the world beyond the frame. For him, what you see is only ever a glimpse of something more diffuse, shadowy, or fleeting. The contingent geometries of his work build on the pioneering projects of many of the artists in this exhibition, who, in various ways, dismantled the limitations of the modernist art object. Although the work of Stella and Truitt that was discussed at the beginning of this essay had already begun to traverse the boundaries between painting and sculpture, artists working from the late 1960s onward conceived of the artwork as more radically dialectical, hybrid, or viral. *Geometries On and Off the Grid* foregrounds this contingency, which remains fundamental to the art of the present.

NOTES

1. Anne Truitt, interview by George and Natalie ("Schatzie") Lee, audio recording, Dallas, TX, April 29, 2002.

2. Frank Stella, "Pratt Lecture" (lecture, Pratt Institute, New York); quoted in Barbara Rose, "ABC Art," *Art in America*, October–November 1965, p. 59.

3. Robert Smithson, *Robert Smithson: The Collected Writings*, ed. Jack Flam (Berkeley and Los Angeles: University of California Press, 1996), p. 240.

4. For an excellent summary of the optical turn in relation to Mono-ha artists such as Sekine Nobuo, see Mika Yoshitake, "The Language of Things: Relation, Perception, and Duration," in *Tokyo, 1955–1970: A New Avant-Garde*, exh. cat. (New York: Museum of Modern Art, 2012), p. 128.

5. Kynaston L. McShine, ed., "Hélio Oiticica," in *Information*, exh. cat. (New York: Museum of Modern Art, 1970), p. 103.

6. Ferreira Gullar et al., "Neo-Concrete Manifesto," reproduced in Mari Carmen Ramírez and Héctor Olea, *Inverted Utopias: Avant-Garde Art in Latin America* (New Haven, CT: Yale University Press, 2014), pp. 496–97.

7. Ferreira Gullar, "Arte neoconcreta: uma contribuicāo brasileiro," in Aracy A. Amaral, *Projecto construtivo brasileiro na arte (1950–1962)* (Rio de Janeiro: Museu de Arte de Moderna do Rio de Janeiro; São Paulo: Pinacoteca do Estado, 1977), p. 115.

8. Lygia Clarke, *Signals Newsbulletin* 1, no. 7 (May–July 1965); quoted in Guy Brett, *Kinetic Art: The Language of Movement* (London and New York: Studio Vista and Reinhold, 1968), p. 61.

9. Bruce Nauman, quoted in Jane Livingston and Marcia Tucker, eds., *Bruce Nauman: Works from 1965 to 1972*, exh. cat. (Los Angeles: Los Angeles County Museum of Art, 1972), p. 11.

10. Robert Pincus-Witten, "Bruce Nauman: Another Kind of Reasoning," *Artforum*, February 1972, p. 33.

11. Nancy Princenthal, *Hannah Wilke* (Munich: Prestel Verlag, 2010), p. 20.

12. Lucy Lippard, "Prefaces to Catalogues of Women's Exhibitions," in *From the Center: Feminist Essays on Women's Art* (New York: Dutton, 1976), p. 49.

13. Bonnie Finnberg, "Body Language: Hannah Wilke Interview," *Cover*, September 1989, p. 16.

14. Joseph Kosuth, interview with Félix González-Torres, in *A. Reinhardt, J. Kosuth, F. González-Torres: Symptoms of Interference, Conditions of Possibility* (London: Art & Design, 1994), pp. 76–81.

15. Ann Goldstein, "Untitled (Ravenswood)," in *Félix González-Torres*, exh. cat. (Los Angeles: Museum of Contemporary Arts, Los Angeles, 1994), p. 40.

16. Mark Bradford, "Remembrance of Things Past(ed)," in *Bounce: Mark Bradford and Glenn Kaino*, exh. cat. (Los Angeles: California Institute of the Arts/REDCAT, 2004), p. 51.

17. Kate Murphy, "Underground Cyberthreats," *New York Times*, November 8, 2015, p. SR6.

18. Christopher Bedford, "Against Abstraction," in *Mark Bradford*, exh. cat. (Columbus, OH: Wexner Center for the Arts, 2010), pp. 24–25.

19. Stella, "Pratt Lecture."

GEOMETRIES ON AND OFF THE GRID
ART FROM 1950 TO THE PRESENT

ALLAN SCHWARTZMAN

GALLERIES 1 AND 2

Minimalism and its artistic predecessors, with their utterly elemental geometric language and monochromatic palettes, seemed an inevitable fulfillment of the broader momentum in modern art toward reduction, a rigorous emptying out of image, illusion, extraneous content, and the authorial cult of gesture. What is left is the essential affirmation of an artwork. Whether the work is veering more toward the material or toward the poetic end of the spectrum, what remains is a grand assertion of a painting simply as "painting" and of the objectness of sculpture.

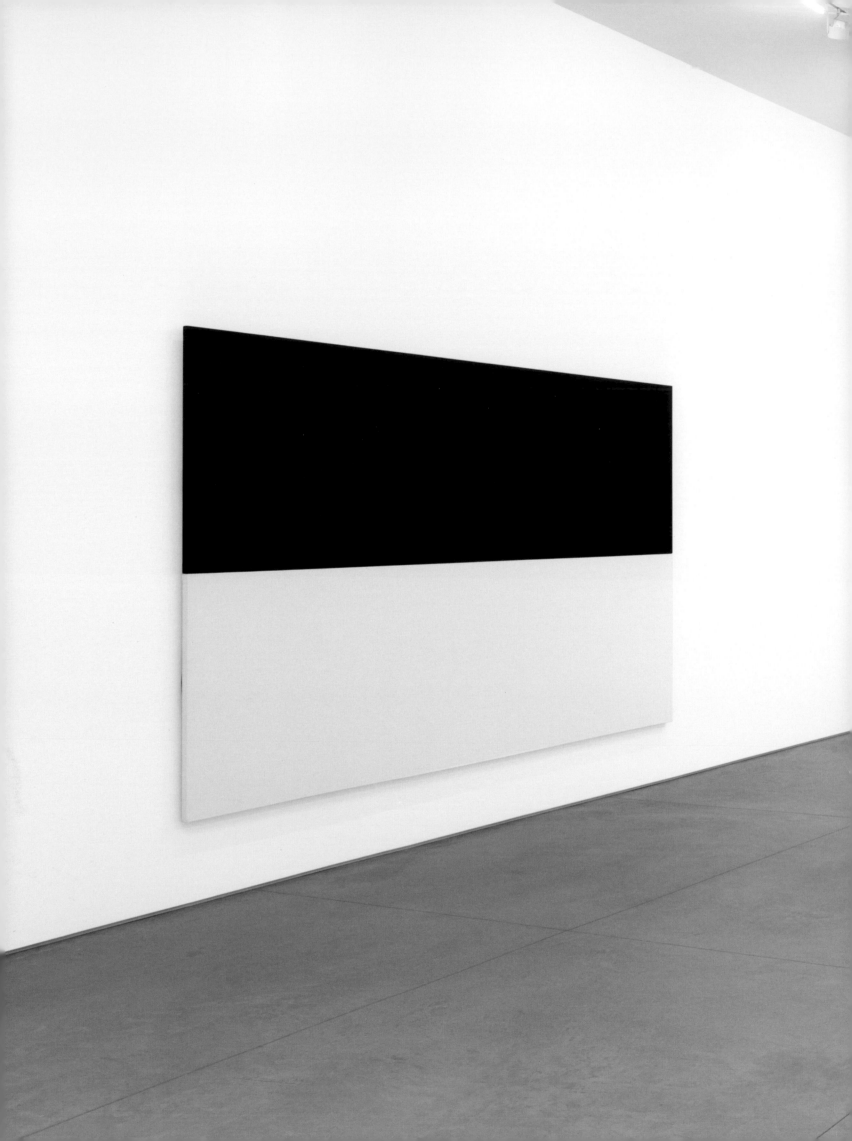

ELLSWORTH KELLY
Sanary, 1952
Oil on wood
51 ½ × 60 in. (130.8 × 152.4 cm)
Collection of Robert and Marguerite Hoffman

AGNES MARTIN
Untitled, 1960
Oil on linen
12 × 12 in. (30.5 × 30.5 cm)
Collection of Robert and Marguerite Hoffman

AGNES MARTIN
Untitled, 1960
Oil on linen
12 × 12 in. (30.5 × 30.5 cm)
The Rachofsky Collection

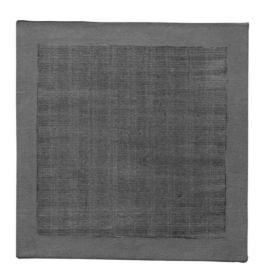

ROBERT RYMAN
Untitled, 1961
Oil paint on stretched linen canvas
37 ⅞ × 37 ⅞ in. (96.2 × 96.2 cm)
The Rachofsky Collection

PIERO MANZONI
Achrome, 1962
Gravel and kaolin on canvas
28 ¾ × 24 ¾ in. (73 × 62.9 cm)
The Rose Collection

FRANK STELLA
Valparaiso Green, 1963
Metallic paint on canvas
78 × 180 in. (198.1 × 457.2 cm)
Collection of Robert and Marguerite Hoffman

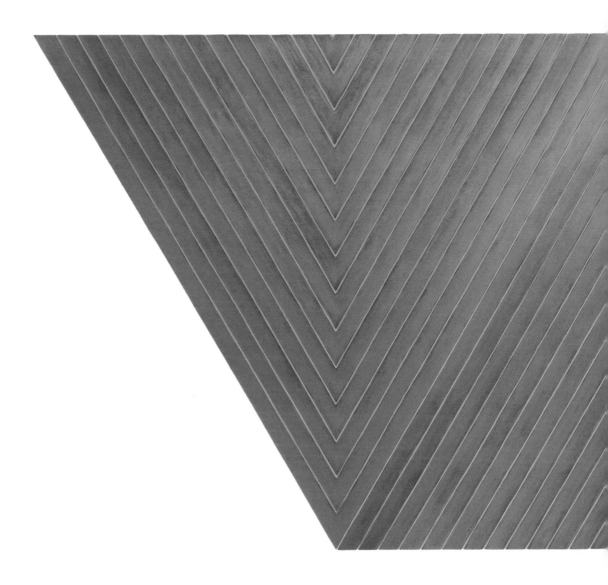

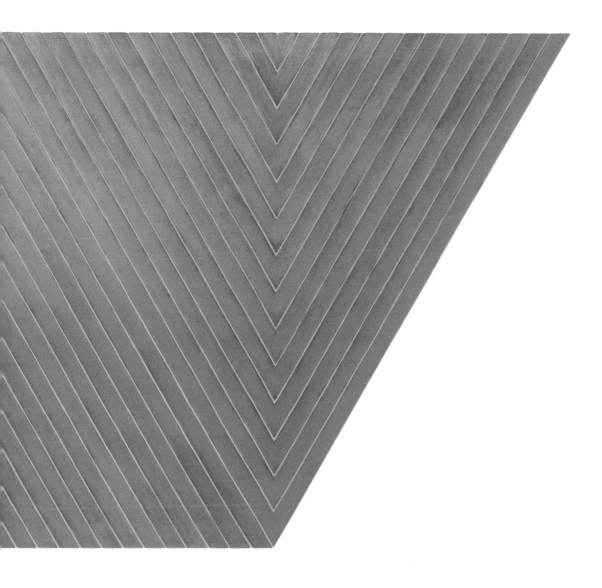

ANNE TRUITT
Valley Forge, 1963
Acrylic on wood
60 ½ × 60 ¼ × 12 in. (153.7 × 153 × 30.5 cm)
The Rachofsky Collection

DAN FLAVIN
alternate diagonals of March 2, 1964 (to Don Judd), March 2, 1964
Daylight and cool white fluorescent tubing
Overall: 144 × 12 in. (365.8 × 30.5 cm)
Dallas Museum of Art, gift of Janie C. Lee

DONALD JUDD
Untitled, 1965
Galvanized iron and brown enamel on aluminum
30 × 150 × 30 in. (76.2 × 381 × 76.2 cm)
Collection of Robert and Marguerite Hoffman

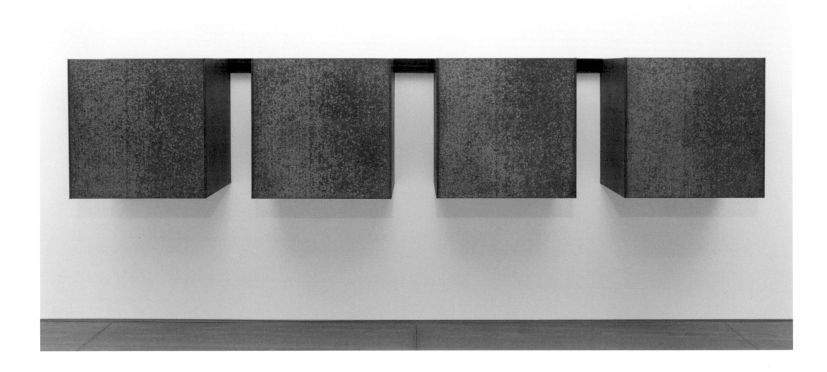

DONALD JUDD
Untitled, 1965
Stainless steel with fluorescent plexiglass
20 × 48 × 34 in. (50.8 × 121.9 × 86.4 cm)
The Rachofsky Collection

CHARLOTTE POSENENSKE
Vierkantrohre (Square Tubes) Series D, 1967/2009, reconstruction
Sheet steel
Installation dimensions variable
The Rose Collection

ELLSWORTH KELLY
Black and White, 1967
Oil on canvas, two joined panels
82 × 144 in. (208.3 × 365.8 cm)
Collection of Robert and Marguerite Hoffman

BARNETT NEWMAN
Untitled Etching I (First Version), 1968
Etching
19 × 29 ½ in. (48.3 × 75 cm)
Edition: 8 of 27
Collection of Marguerite Steed Hoffman

DONALD JUDD
Untitled, 1970
Clear and purple anodized aluminum
Overall: 8 ¼ × 253 ⅜ × 8 ¼ in. (21 × 643.6 × 21 cm)
Dallas Museum of Art, fractional gift of The Rachofsky Collection

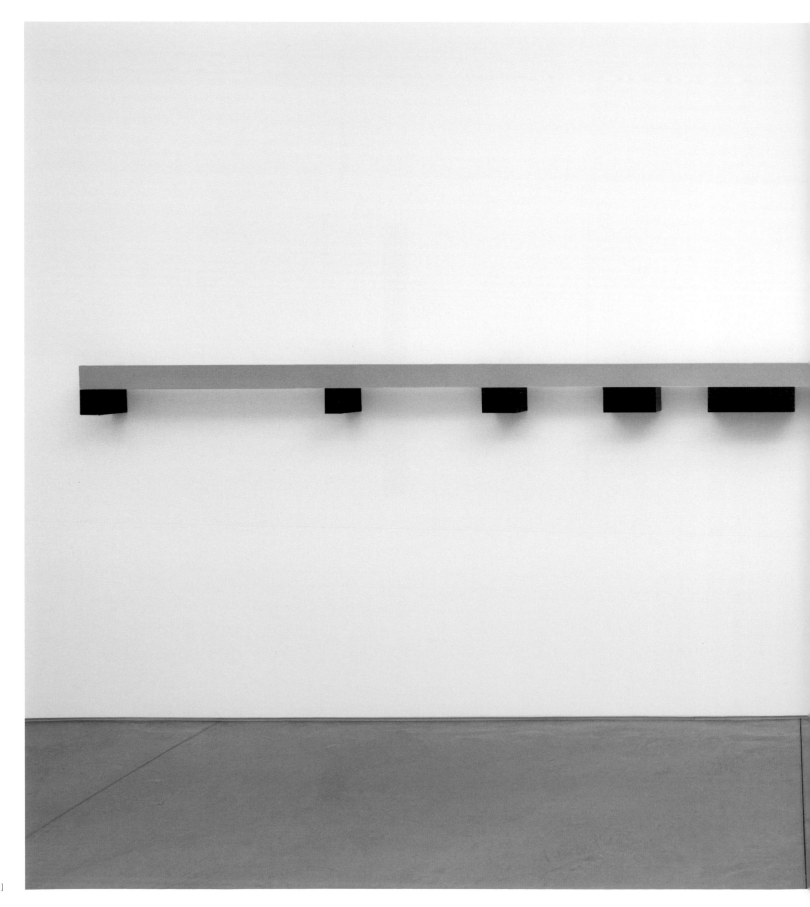

ELLSWORTH KELLY
Two Grays I, 1975
Oil on canvas, two joined panels
92 × 102 in. (233.7 × 259.1 cm)
Collection of Robert and Marguerite Hoffman

AGNES MARTIN
Untitled #1, 1993
Acrylic and graphite on canvas
60 × 60 in. (152.4 × 152.4 cm)
The Rachofsky Collection

GALLERY 3

Inevitably, such an exquisite reduction of art to its physical essence was also its exquisite undoing. Later in the 1960s and early 1970s, geometry breaks apart, painting loses the structure of the stretcher, and sculpture begins to be defined by a tenuous relationship of opposing materials and physical dependencies and to fracture into the immeasurable subjectivity of perception. The material gives way to the ephemeral. Spiritually and literally, artists begin to leave the shelter of the frame, the wall, and the studio.

RICHARD TUTTLE
Sail, 1964
Acrylic on wood
10 × 40 × 3 in. (25.4 × 101.6 × 7.6 cm)
The Rose Collection

RICHARD TUTTLE
Equals, 1964–65
Acrylic on plywood
39 × 47 ¾ × 1 ½ in. (99.1 × 120 × 3.8 cm)
Collection of Robert and Marguerite Hoffman

ROBERT SMITHSON
Ziggurat, 1966
Painted and polished metal
27 ½ × 27 ½ × 24 in. (69.9 × 69.9 × 61 cm)
The Rose Collection

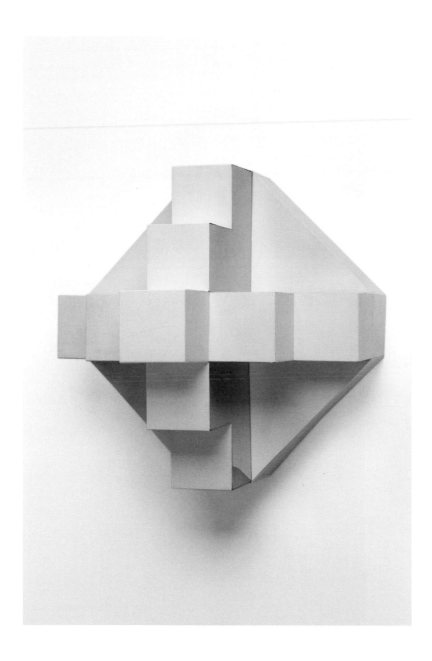

GIOVANNI ANSELMO
Senza titolo (*Untitled*), 1967
Wood, water, and Formica
63 × 23 ⅝ × 23 ⅝ in. (160 × 60 × 60 cm)
The Rachofsky Collection

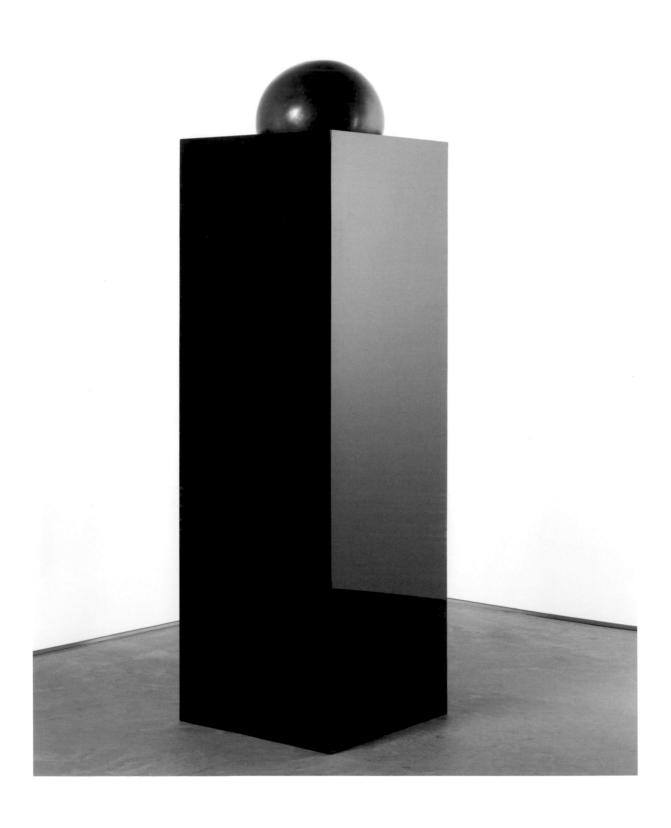

GIANNI PIACENTINO
Metalloid Violet-Blue Vertical Wedge-Shaped Object (III), 1967–68
Polyester-coated and painted (water-base enamel, 2K acrylic matt
clear) wood
114 ¼ × 4 × 15 ¾ in. (290 × 10 × 40 cm)
Collection of Marguerite Steed Hoffman

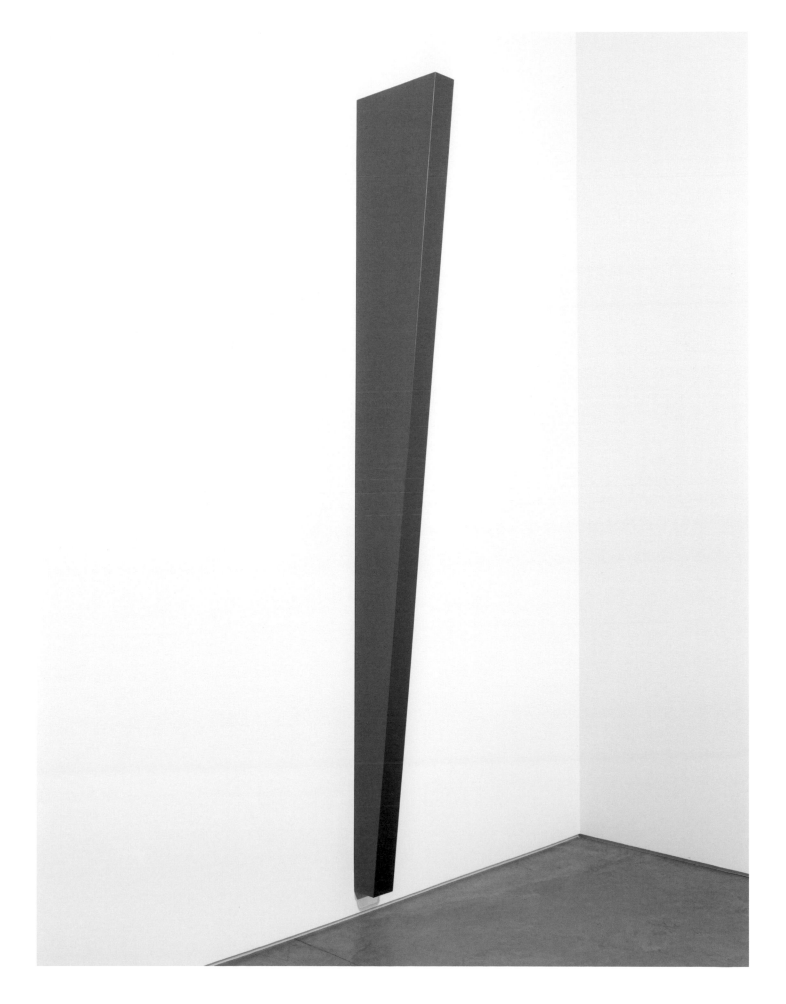

ALAN SARET
Green Wave of Air, 1968–69
Chicken wire
54 × 60 × 46 in. (137.2 × 152.4 × 116.8 cm)
Collection of Marguerite Steed Hoffman

RICHARD SERRA
Close Pin Prop, 1969–76
Rolled lead
Tube: 48 × 12 in. (121.9 × 30.5 cm)
Pole: 96 × 8 in. (243.8 × 20.3 cm)
The Rachofsky Collection

ROBERT SMITHSON
Mirrors and Shelly Sand, 1969–70
Mirrors and beach sand with shells or pebbles
Fifty mirrors, back to back, each: 12 × 48 in. (30.5 × 121.9 cm)
Installation length: approximately 28 ft. (8.5 m)
Dallas Museum of Art, gift of an anonymous donor; the Vin and Caren
Prothro Foundation; Rusty and Deedie Rose in memory of Vin Prothro
and in honor of his cherished grandchildren, Lillian Lee Clark and
Annabel Caren Clark; The Eugene McDermott Foundation; Dr. and Mrs.
Mark L. Lemmon; American Consolidated Media; Bear/Hunter; and
donors to the C. Vincent Prothro Memorial Foundation

NOBUO SEKINE
Phase of Nothingness—Cloth and Stone, 1970/1994
Cloth, stone, rope, and panel
94 ½ × 89 ½ × 7 ⅞ in. (240 × 227.3 × 20 cm)
The Rachofsky Collection and the Dallas Museum of Art
through the DMA/amfAR Benefit Auction Fund

RICHARD TUTTLE
1st Wire Bridge, 1971
Wire and nails
37 ½ × 38 ½ in. (95.2 × 97.8 cm)
The Rachofsky Collection

TONY CONRAD
Yellow Movie 2/26/73, 1973
Emulsion: Empire Yellow Gloss Enamel by Eaglo, odorless Magicote
Base: White canvas, stretched
Screen: 24 × 33 in. (61 × 83.8 cm)
Overall: 33 × 42 in. (83.8 × 106.7 cm)
The Rose Collection

MICHAEL HEIZER
Untitled #2, 1975
Polyvinyl, latex, and aluminum powder on canvas
Diameter: 96 in. (243.8 cm)
The Rose Collection

ROBERT IRWIN
Little Jazz, 2010
Light + Shadow + Reflection + Color
72 × 81 ⅜ × 4 ⅝ in. (182.9 × 206.7 × 11.7 cm)
Amy and Vernon Faulconer and The Rachofsky Collection

GALLERY 4

The road to reductionism is rooted in European Constructivism. After World War II, artists in Europe, the United States, and Latin America, many of them European by birth, find ways to assert the flatness and the physical essence of painting. Ultimately, they reposition painting as a conceptual exploration, not an esthetic one, the change apparent early in Piero Manzoni's stitched velvet *Achrome*, 1960 (p. 100 and detail, p. 83), and Yves Klein's *Untitled Monogold*, 1961 (p. 101), and later in Gerhard Richter's *Farbtafel* (*Colour Chart*), 1966 (p. 107).

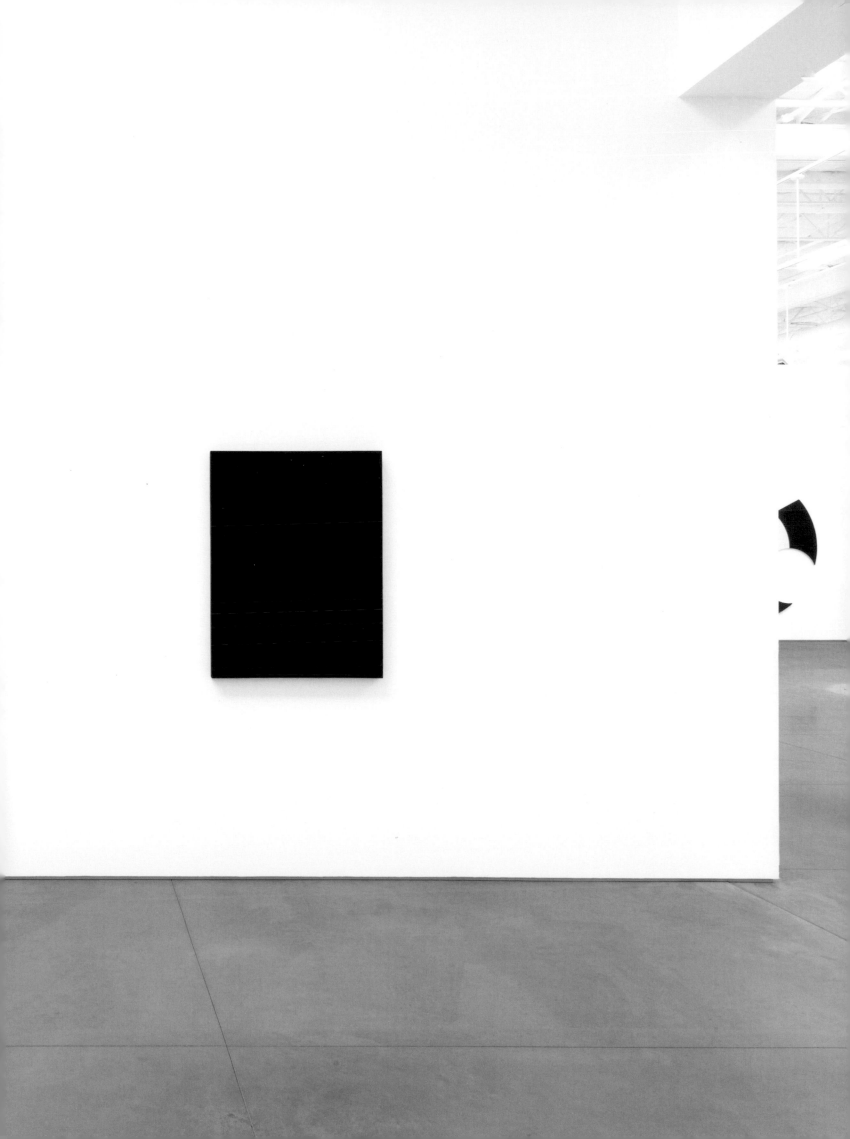

TONY SMITH
Untitled, c. 1934–36
Oil on canvas board
9 × 7 in. (22.9 × 17.8 cm)
The Rose Collection

AD REINHARDT
Untitled (black diptych), 1959–60
Oil on canvas
40 × 30 in. (101.6 × 76.2 cm)
The Rachofsky Collection

PIERO MANZONI
Achrome, 1960
Stitched velvet and board
31 ¼ × 23 ⅜ in. (79.4 × 59.4 cm)
The Rachofsky Collection

YVES KLEIN
Untitled Monogold, 1961
Gold leaf on panel
24 ⅜ × 17 ¾ in. (62 × 45 cm)
Collection of Marguerite Steed Hoffman

JOSEF ALBERS
Homage to the Square (732), 1961
Oil on Masonite
Panel: 30½ × 30½ in. (76.5 × 76.5 cm)
Framed: 30½ × 30½ × 1½ in. (77.8 × 77.8 × 3.2 cm)
Dallas Museum of Art, gift of Anni Albers and the
Josef Albers Foundation, Inc.

LYGIA PAPE
Livro Noite e Dia (Book Night and Day), 1963–76
Tempera on wood
Twelve pieces, each: 6 ¼ × 6 ¼ in. (15.9 × 15.9 cm)
The Rose Collection

MIRA SCHENDEL
Untitled, 1963
Tempera on canvas
31 ⅞ × 39 ¾ in. (81 × 101 cm)
The Rose Collection

MIRA SCHENDEL
Untitled, 1964
Plaster and tempera on wooden board
16½ × 13¾ × 1 in. (42 × 35 × 2.5 cm)
The Rose Collection

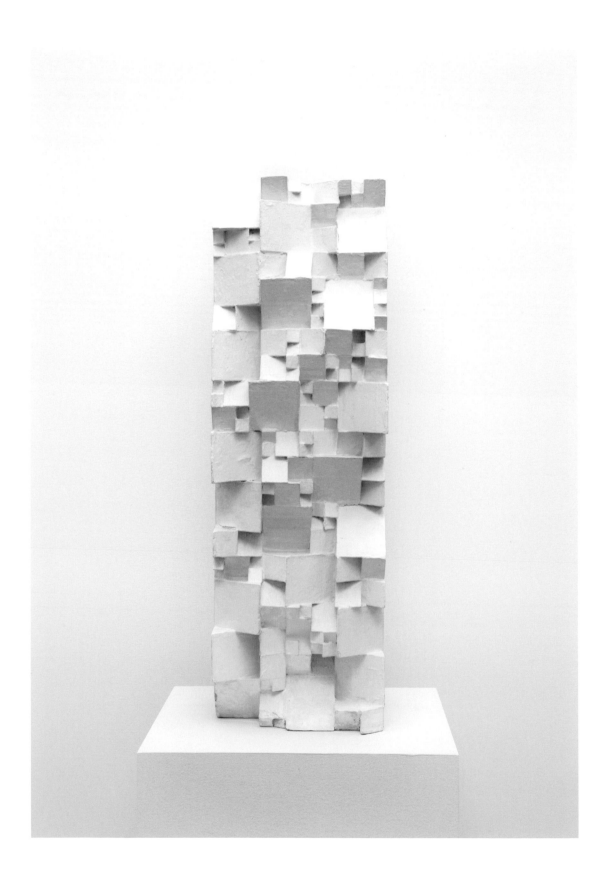

GERHARD RICHTER
Farbtafel (*Colour Chart*), 1966
Enamel on canvas
29½ × 19¾ in. (75 × 50 cm)
The Rose Collection

GALLERY 5

As American artists working in the 1950s and 1960s were affirming an immaculate perfection and the dependability of geometry, artists elsewhere were exploring imperfect geometries, the unraveling of their certainty and, ultimately, the disintegration of the object itself. Lucio Fontana redefines a simple line as a cut into immeasurable space, both visually and metaphysically; Manzoni leaves the formation of a network of lines to the happenstance of process; Blinky Palermo faintly veils his somewhat asymmetrically placed triangles; and Mira Schendel in her plastic *Transformável* (*Transformable*), 1970 (p. 130 and detail, p. 111), creates an ambling line that is representative not so much of its barely perceptible existence as of its conditionally measurable shadow.

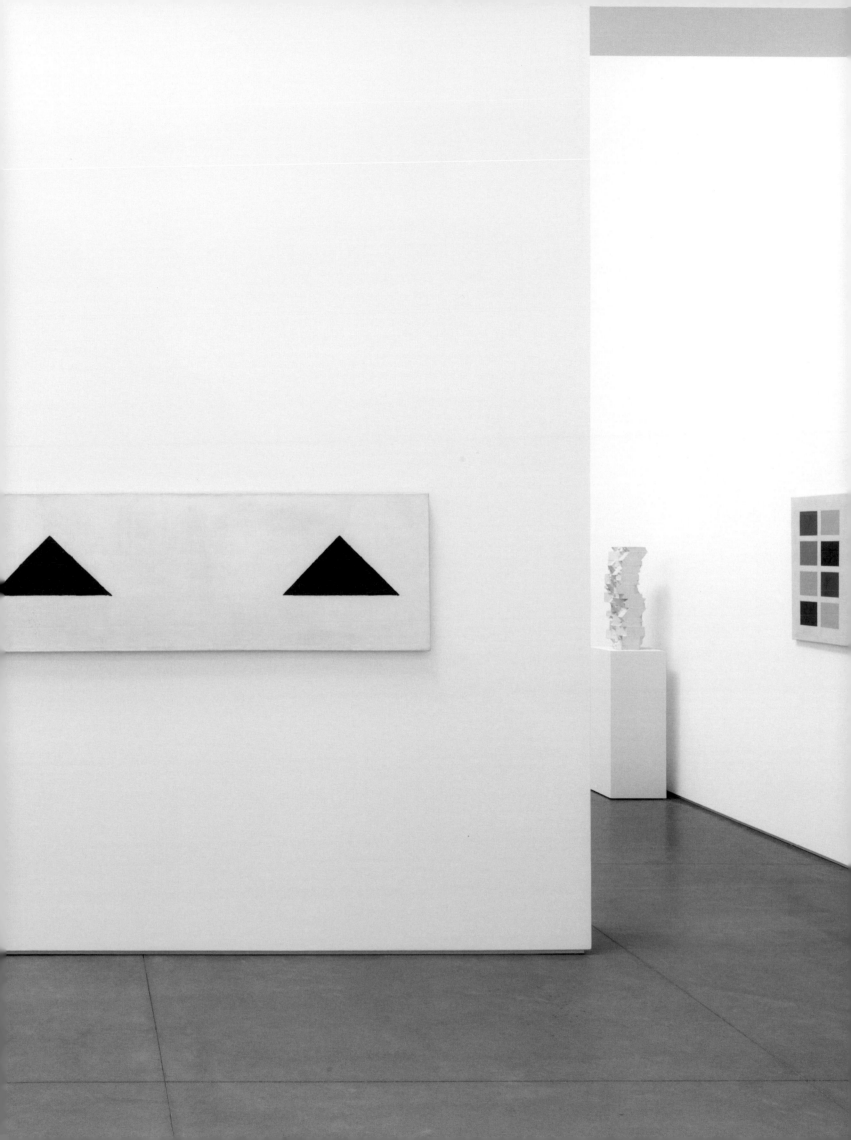

LEON POLK SMITH
Black angles on white, 1947
Oil on canvas mounted on plywood
Panel: 36 × 12 in. (91.4 × 30.5 cm)
Canvas: 33 ¼ × 8 ¾ in. (84.5 × 22.2 cm)
The Rose Collection

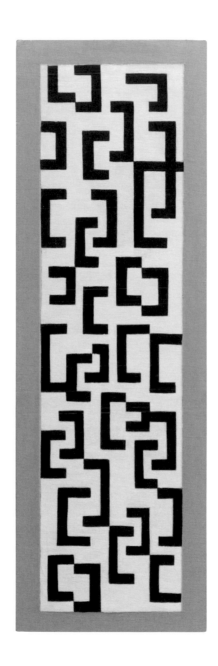

CHARLOTTE POSENENSKE
Rasterbild (Halbkreise) (Grid [*Semi-circles*]), 1957
Study for a piece of wall art
Pencil on paper
15 ⅜ × 21 ⅞ in. (39 × 55.5 cm)
The Rose Collection

CHARLOTTE POSENENSKE
Rasterbild (Halbkreise) (Grid [*Semi-circles*]), 1957
Flat model for a wall relief in the Dieburg District Court,
horizontal rows of recessed circles with systematically varied,
embossed semi-circle segments (not realized)
15 × 24 ½ in. (38 × 62 cm)
The Rose Collection

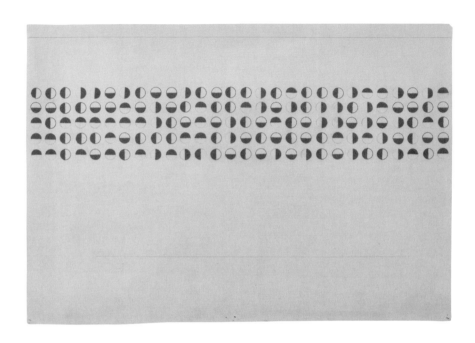

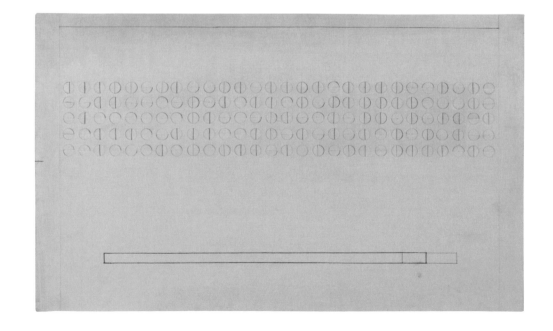

PIERO MANZONI
Achrome, 1958
Kaolin on canvas
38 ¾ × 51 ⅛ in. (98.4 × 129.9 cm)
The Rachofsky Collection

MIRA SCHENDEL
Untitled, 1960s
Oil transfer drawing on thin Japanese paper
between painted transparent acrylic sheets
19⅝ × 19⅝ in. (49.8 × 49.8 cm)
Collection of Marguerite Steed Hoffman

LUCIO FONTANA
Concetto spaziale, Attesa (Spatial Concept, Expectation), 1964
Waterpaint on canvas
45 ⅝ × 31 ⅞ in. (115.9 × 81 cm)
The Rachofsky Collection

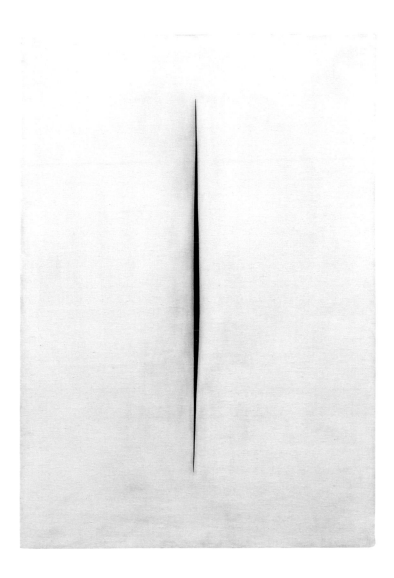

VICTOR GRIPPO
Sin título (*Untitled*), 1965
Oil on canvas
35 ½ × 19 ¾ in. (90.2 × 50.2 cm)
The Rose Collection

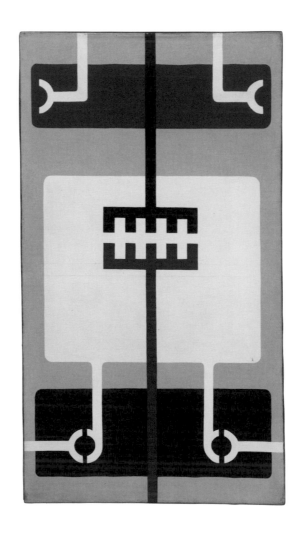

ALIGHIERO BOETTI
Zig Zag, 1966
Fabric and aluminum
19 ⅝ × 19 ⅝ × 19 ⅝ in. (49.8 × 49.8 × 49.8 cm)
The Rose Collection

NORIO IMAI
White Ceremony/Toward #1, 1966–70
Acrylic, cotton cloth, and plastic pattern
28 ½ × 15 ½ × 3 ⅛ in. (72.5 × 39.5 × 8 cm)
The Rachofsky Collection

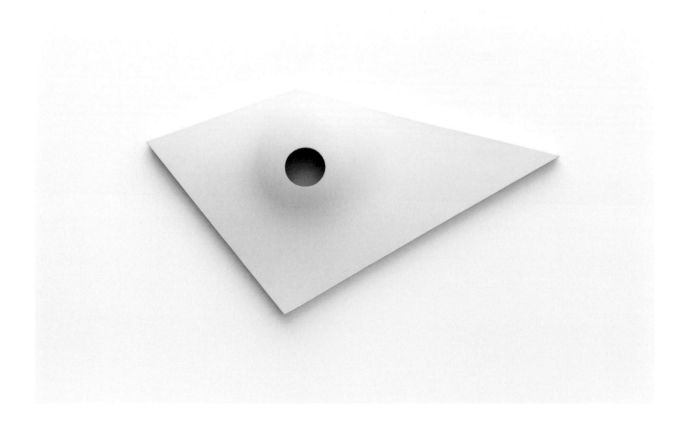

BLINKY PALERMO
Untitled, 1967–68
Casein paint on canvas
23 ⅝ × 70 ½ in. (60 × 180 cm)
The Rose Collection

MIRA SCHENDEL
Transformável (Transformable), 1970
Riveted strips of transparent acrylic
Approximately 25 ⅝ in. (65 cm)
The Rose Collection

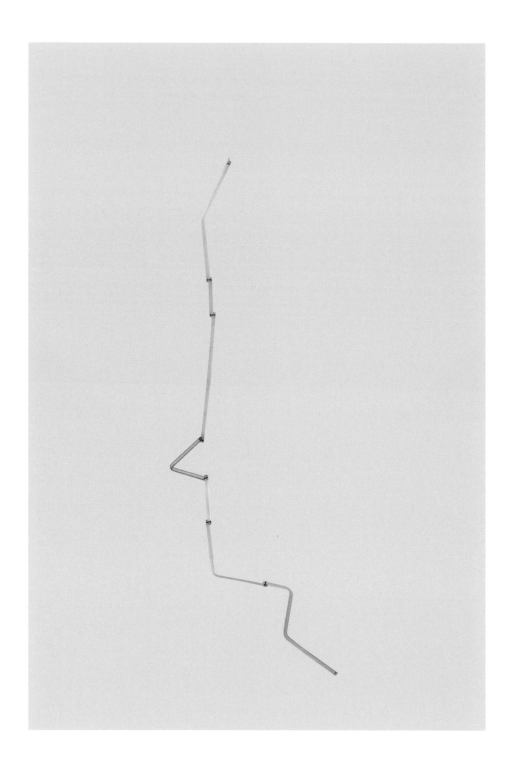

JIRO TAKAMATSU
Shadow of Nail No. 400, 1975
Lacquer and iron nail on wood panel
12 ⅞ × 9 ¼ in. (32.7 × 23.5 cm)
The Rachofsky Collection

GALLERY 6

Outside the artistic center of New York, geometric order starts to disintegrate sooner. In the early 1950s, for Shozo Shimamoto in Japan and Mimmo Rotella in Italy, both places where the devastation of war was still part of daily life, art becomes reduced to the gritty materiality of the aftermath, an indefiniteness made intentionally visual. In Brazil, Lygia Clark, in her quest to break the authority of the frame of painting, fractures and manipulates geometry, finding her way from painting to sculpture. By the mid- and late 1960s, the art object becomes twisted, bent, folded, wedged apart, fragmented, chopped up, and then reassembled. Its order is disrupted. Paralleling broader social, political, and sexual revolutions around the world, circles and squares are being splayed open and split apart, form is being intentionally dissected, and artists are dissenting from the dogma of the formal and the authority it embodies. They are still working principally within the language of abstraction, but now with an underlying sense of psychological, metaphysical, and political rebellion against the patriarchal order of geometry.

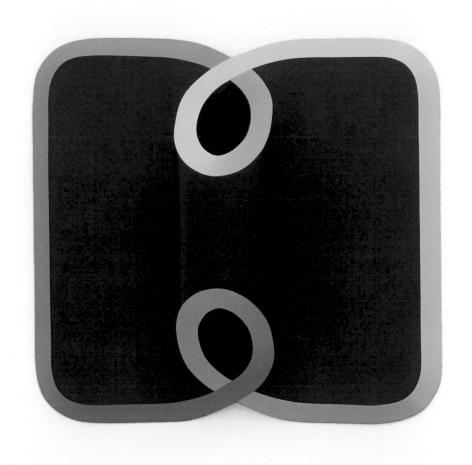

SHOZO SHIMAMOTO
Work-(Hole 05)-, 1950
White paint on newspaper
19¾ × 13¾ in. (49 × 35 cm)
The Rose Collection

MIMMO ROTELLA
Senza titolo (*Untitled*), 1954
Back of poster
23 ⅝ × 21 ⅝ in. (60 × 54.9 cm)
The Rachofsky Collection

LYGIA CLARK
Casulo (Cocoon), 1959
Acrylic paint, balsam, and graphite
5 ¼ × 5 ¼ in. (13.3 × 13.3 cm)
The Rose Collection

LYGIA CLARK
Bicho—Em si (Creature—In Itself), 1962
Aluminum
12 ¼ × 9 ⅞ × 8 ⅝ in. (31.1 × 25.1 × 21.9 cm)
Installation dimensions variable
The Rose Collection

LYGIA CLARK
Estruturas de caixa de fósforos (*Matchbox Structures*), 1964
Gouache paint, matchboxes, and glue
3 ⅛ × 5 ½ × 2 in. (7.9 × 14 × 5.1 cm)
The Rose Collection

RICHARD ARTSCHWAGER
Swivel, 1964
Formica on wood
53 ⅜ × 25 ½ × 30 ¾ in. (135.6 × 64.8 × 78.1 cm)
The Rose Collection and The Rachofsky Collection

JIRO YOSHIHARA
Work, 1965
Oil on canvas
71 × 90 in. (180.3 × 228.6 cm)
The Rachofsky Collection

BRUCE NAUMAN
Untitled (Lead Piece with Wedge), 1968
Lead, steel, and paint
4 × 47¼ × 47¼ in. (10.2 × 120 × 120 cm)
Dallas Museum of Art, anonymous gift

NOBUO SEKINE
Phase No. 10, 1968
Wood, oil-based paint, and FRP
68 ½ × 72 ½ × 24 ¾ in. (174 × 184 × 63 cm)
The Rachofsky Collection and the Dallas Museum of Art
through the DMA/amfAR Benefit Auction Fund

JIRO TAKAMATSU
Cube 6 + 3, 1968
Lacquer on wood
13 × 13 × 13 in. (33 × 33 × 33 cm)
The Rachofsky Collection and the Dallas Museum of Art
through the DMA/amfAR Benefit Auction Fund

JIRO TAKAMATSU
Oneness of Paper, 1970
Colored paper on Kent paper
24 ⅜ × 16 in. (62 × 40.5 cm)
The Rachofsky Collection and the Dallas Museum of Art,
gift of Mrs. Jiro Takamatsu

CILDO MEIRELES
Espelho Cego (*Blind Mirror*), 1970
Wood, rubber, and reversed metal in text relief
19 ¼ × 14 ⅛ × 7 ⅛ in. (48.9 × 35.9 × 18.1 cm)
1 of 3 versions
The Rose Collection

HÉLIO OITICICA
Untitled, 1970
Four shades of yellow ink on wood
33 ½ × 34 ⅝ × 41 ⅜ in. (85 × 88 × 105 cm)
The Rose Collection

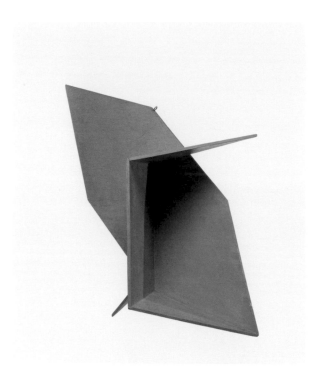

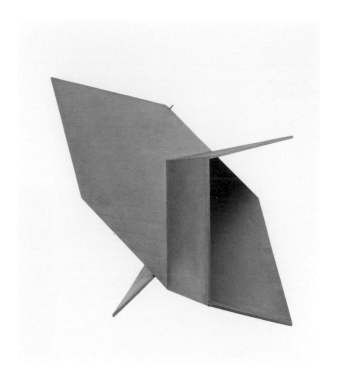

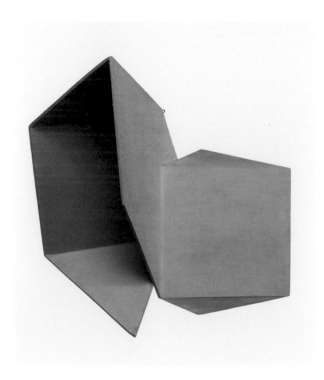

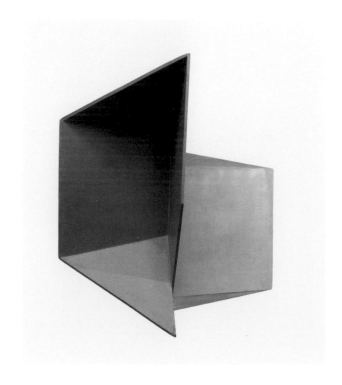

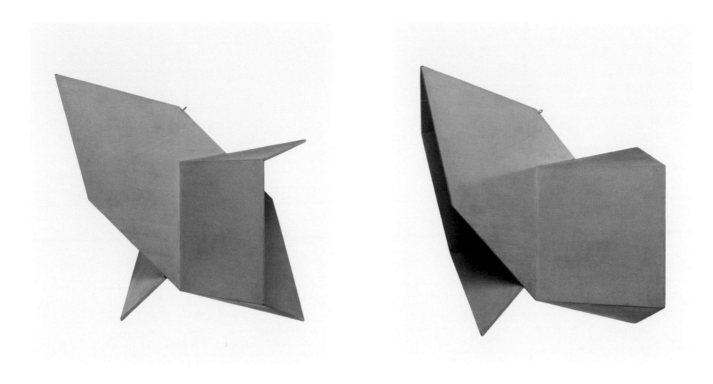

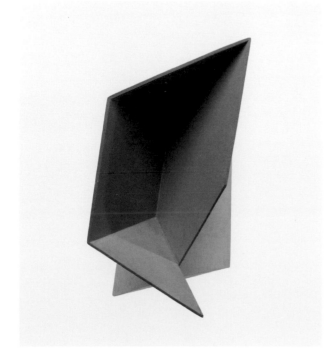

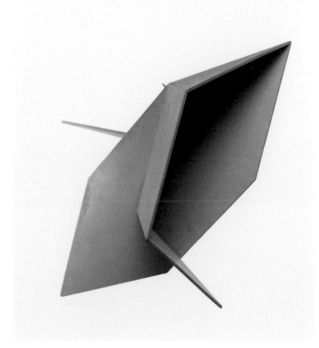

REE MORTON
Wood Drawings, 1971
Felt-tip pen, pencil, acrylic, clay, sponge, and hardware on wood
Sixteen drawings—height (range): 2 ½ to 17 ½ in. (6.3 to 44.4 cm);
length (range): 6 to 34 in. (15.2 to 86.4 cm)
The Rose Collection

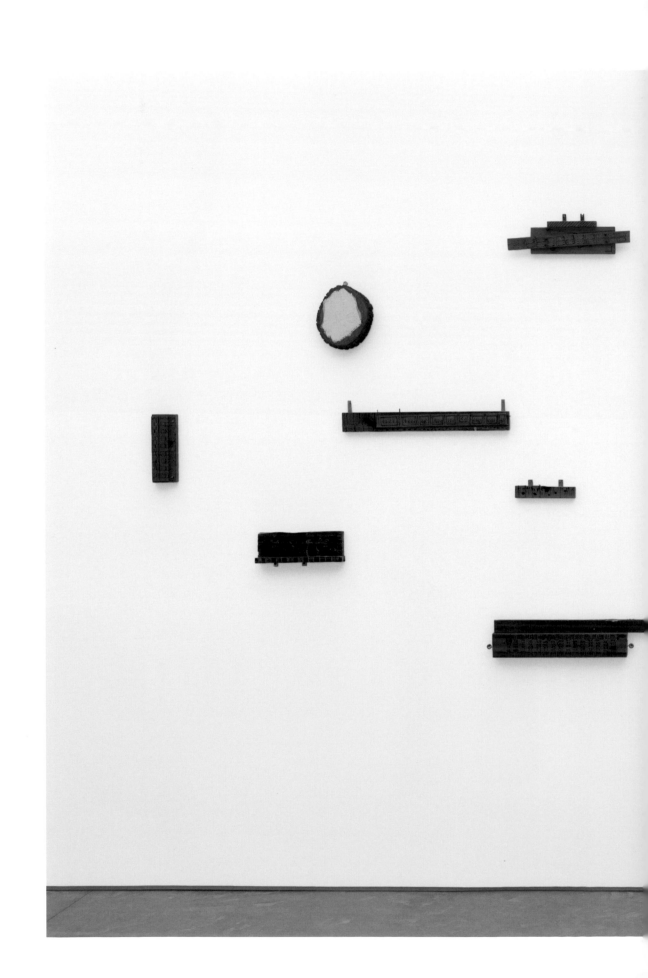

GORDON MATTA-CLARK
Bronx Floors: Floor above, ceiling below, 1973
Gelatin silver prints
Two prints, framed: 26 ¾ × 20 ¾ in. (67.9 × 52.7 cm)
The Rose Collection

PAULO ROBERTO LEAL
Des-Mov-Em, c. 1974
Acrylic box and rice paper
11 ¾ × 7 ⅞ × 7 ⅞ in. (29.8 × 20 × 20 cm)
The Rose Collection

VICTOR GRIPPO
Vida, Muerte, Resurrección (Life, Death, Resurrection), 1980
Five hollow geometrical lead bodies; five hollow geometrical lead
bodies filled with black and red beans; water; glass box
Overall: 19½ × 47½ × 31½ in. (49.5 × 120.6 × 80 cm)
The Rose Collection

JOHN CHAMBERLAIN
Rap Psalm II, 1999
Painted chromium and painted steel
103 ½ × 59 × 47 in. (262.9 × 149.9 × 119.4 cm)
The Rachofsky Collection

ROBERT RYMAN
Lift, 2002
Oil on linen
43 × 43 in. (109.2 × 109.2 cm)
The Rose Collection

GALLERIES 7 AND 9

For many artists, the disintegration of the shelter of geometry provides fresh ways to explore composition, mark making, and the possibilities of what can be a painting. The measurable gives way to a wider perceptual field. Transcendence finds a new way back into painting. Even when geometric perfection remains, the definitive importance of the edge collapses and, as exemplified in Robert Irwin's sculptural disk, the perceptual experience of the work extends beyond the physical limits of the object.

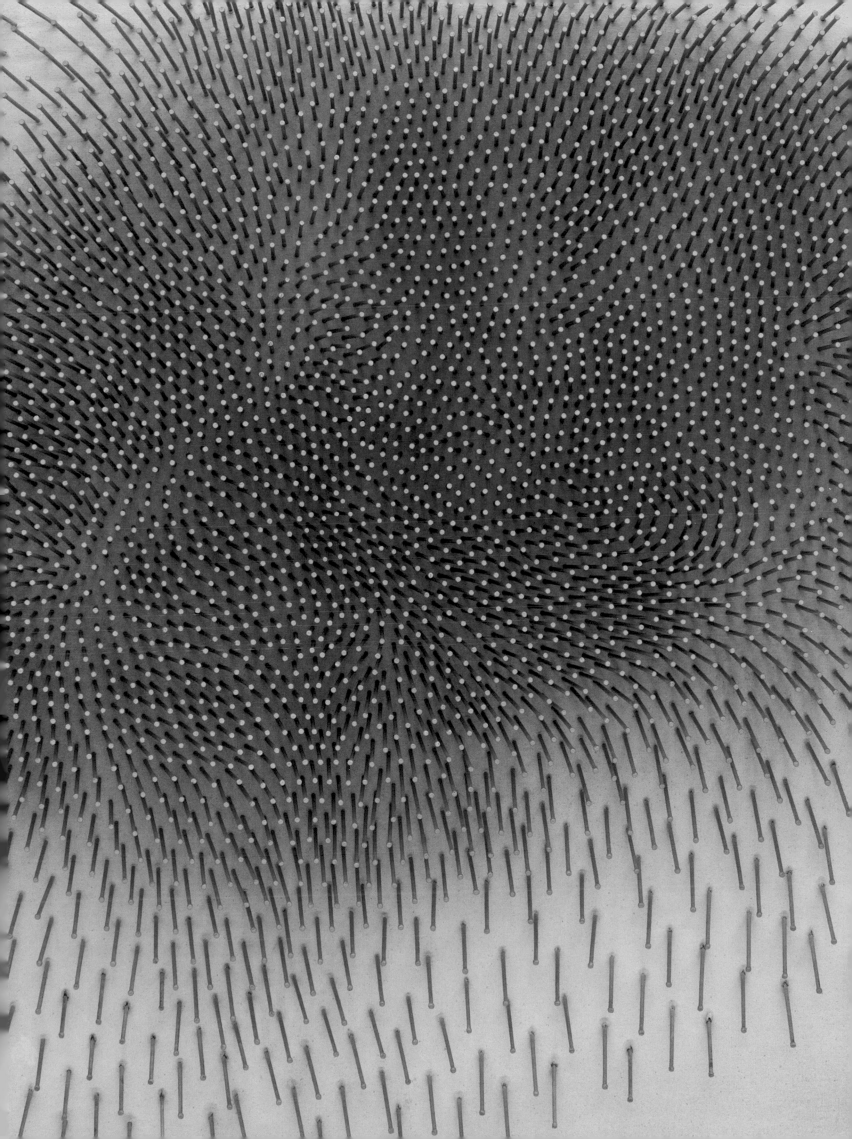

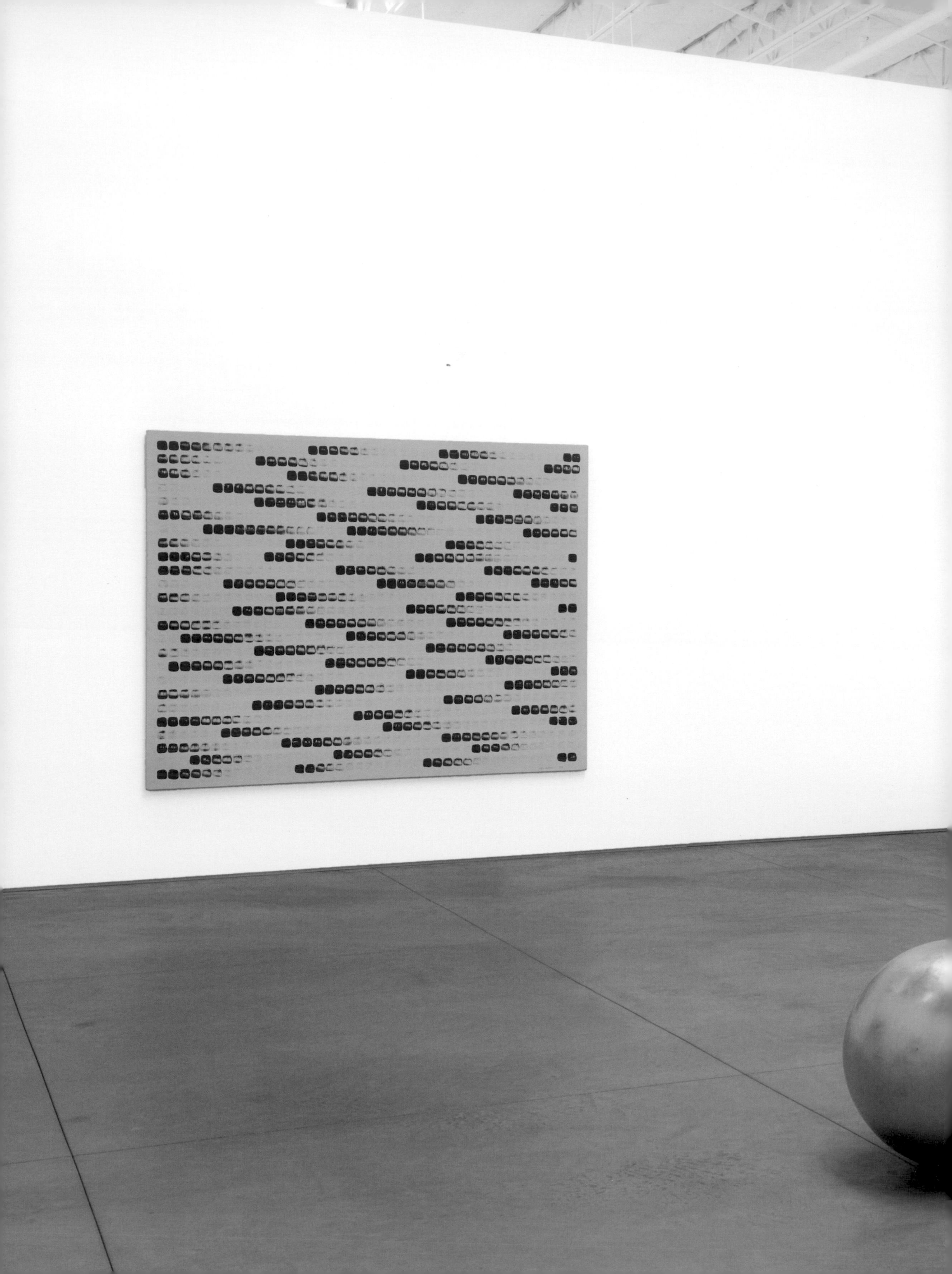

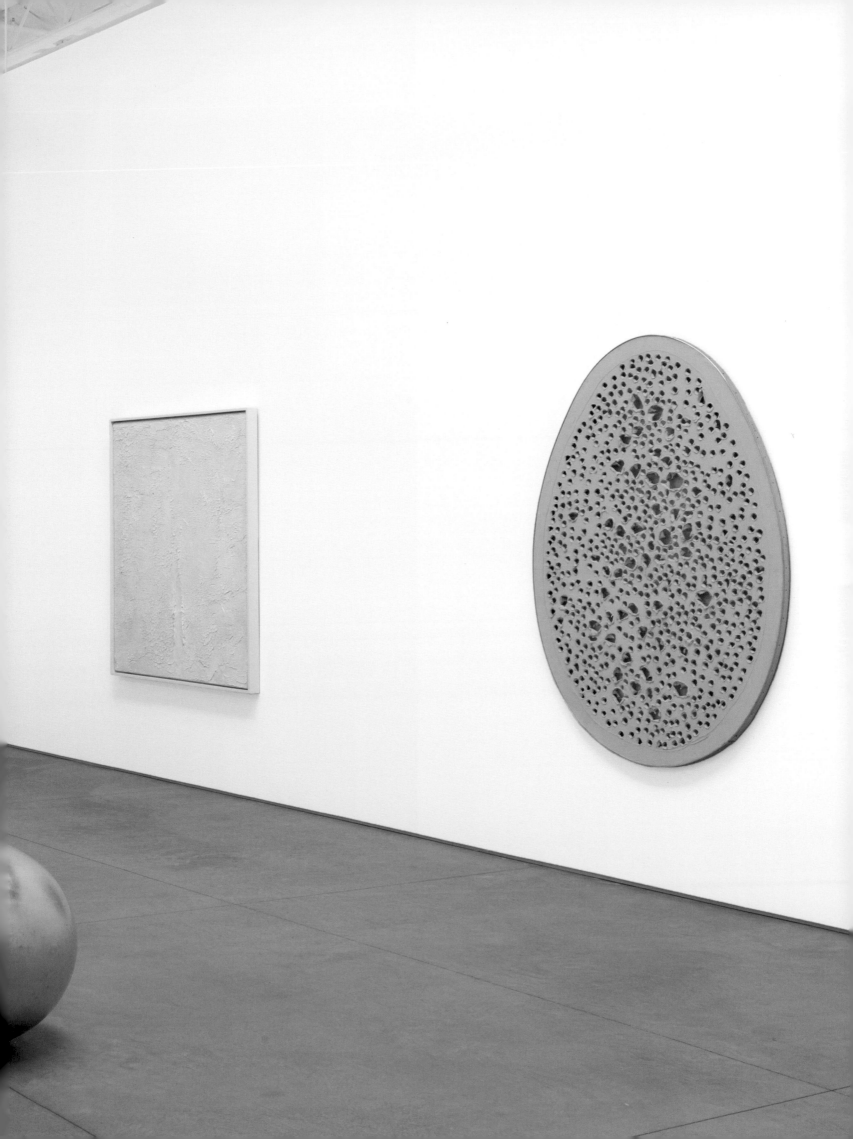

DADAMAINO
Volume a modulazioni sfasate (Volume of Displaced Modules), 1960
Sheets of plastic applied on superimposed frames
15 ¾ × 11 ¾ in. (40 × 30 cm)
The Rose Collection

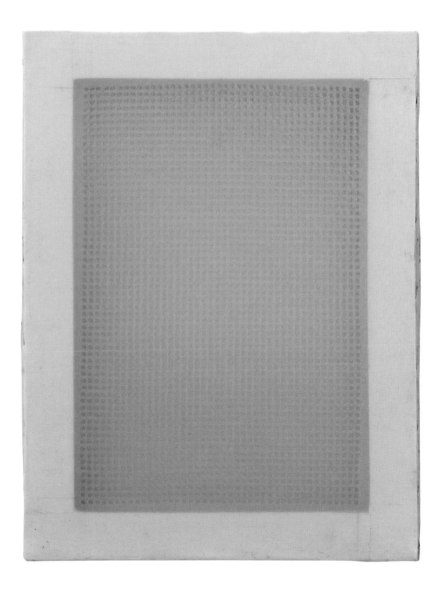

GÜNTHER UECKER
Weisses Phantom, 1962
Painted nails and oil on canvas on panel
43 ⅜ × 78 ¾ in. (110.2 × 200 cm)
The Rachofsky Collection

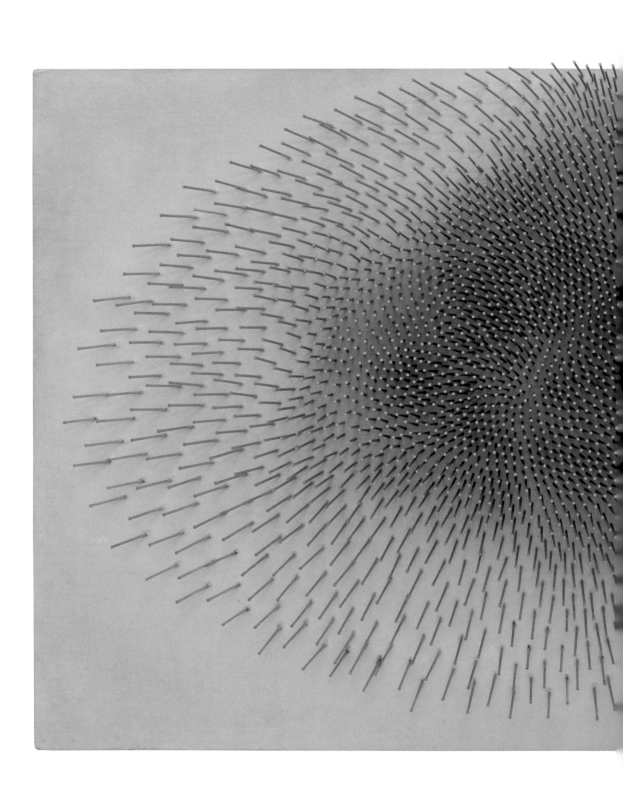

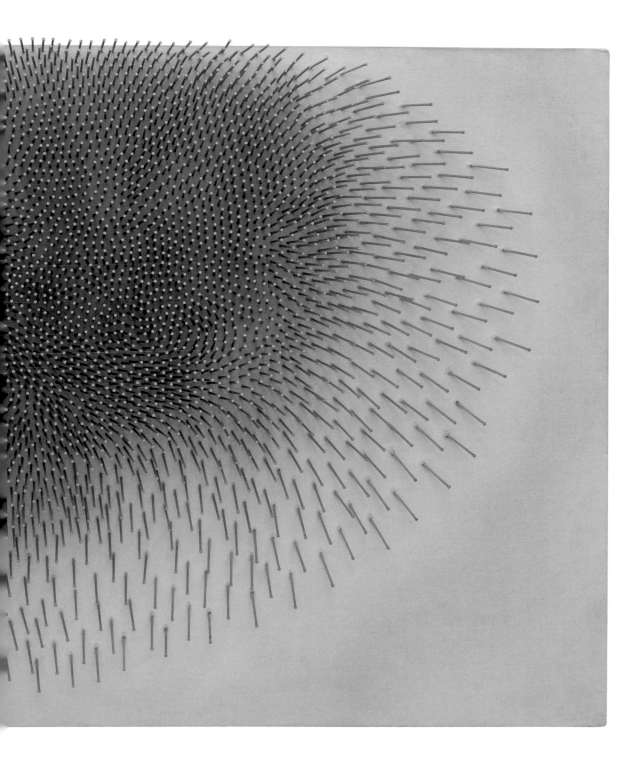

LUCIO FONTANA
Concetto spaziale, la fine di Dio (Spatial Concept, The End of God), 1964
Oil on canvas
70 × 48½ in. (177.8 × 123.2 cm)
The Rachofsky Collection

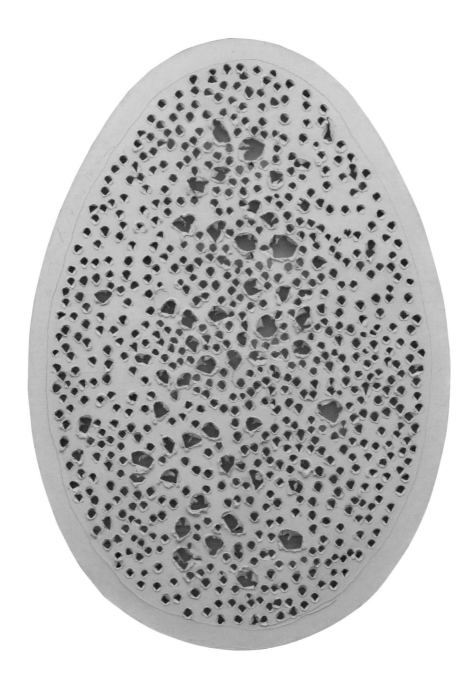

MARCEL BROODTHAERS
Ovale d'oeufs 1234567 (Oval of eggs 1234567), 1965
Eggshells and oil paint on wood panel
39 ⅜ × 31 ½ × 4 ¾ in. (100 × 80 × 12.1 cm)
Dallas Museum of Art, fractional gift of The Rachofsky Collection

ENRICO CASTELLANI
Superficie Blu (*Blue Surface*), 1965
Oil on canvas
72 × 107 ¾ in. (182.9 × 273.7 cm)
The Rachofsky Collection

PETER ALEXANDER
Pink Green Cube, 1967
Cast polyester resin
8 × 8 × 8 in. (20.3 × 20.3 × 20.3 cm)
Pedestal: 45 × 14 × 14 in. (114.3 × 35.6 × 35.6 cm)
The Rose Collection

ROBERT IRWIN
Untitled, 1968–69
Acrylic lacquer on formed acrylic plastic
Diameter: 54 in. (137.2 cm)
Dallas Museum of Art, fractional gift of The Rachofsky Collection

SERGIO CAMARGO
Relief No. 262, 1969
Wood relief and paint
Panel: 47 ¼ × 39 ⅜ × 3 ⅛ in. (120 × 100 × 7.9 cm)
Dallas Museum of Art, gift of Mr. and Mrs. James H. Clark

ALBERTO BURRI
Cretto B2, 1973
Acrovinyl on cellotex
59 × 49¾ in. (149.9 × 125.1 cm)
The Rachofsky Collection

LEE UFAN
From Point, 1978
Glue and stone pigment on canvas
71 ½ × 89 ⅜ in. (181.6 × 227 cm)
The Rachofsky Collection and the Dallas Museum of Art
through the DMA/amfAR Benefit Auction Fund

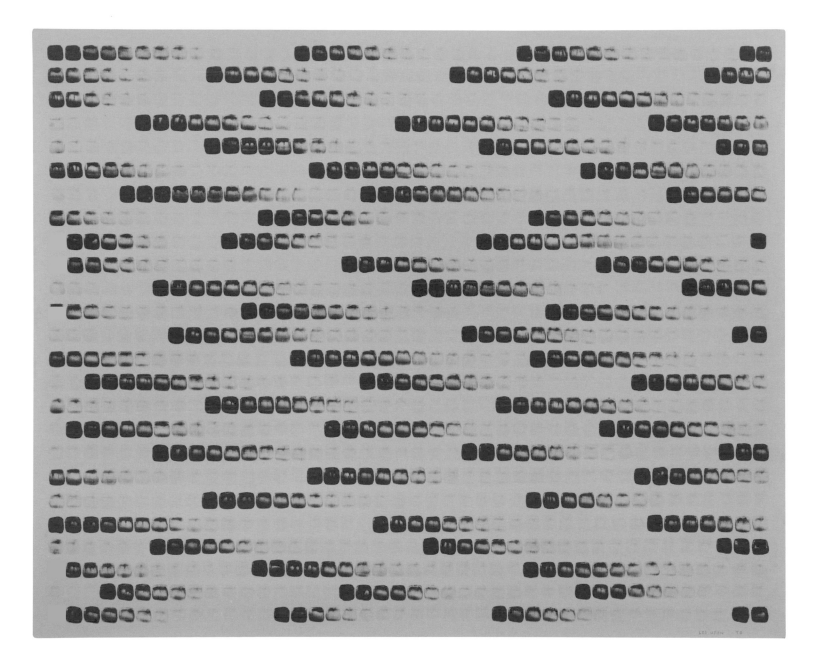

JAMES LEE BYARS
Is, 1989
Gilded marble
Diameter: 23 ½ in. (59.7 cm)
Collection of Marguerite Steed Hoffman

ROBERT RYMAN
Series #9 (White), 2004
Oil on canvas
53 × 53 in. (134.6 × 134.6 cm)
The Rachofsky Collection

GALLERY 8

Reduced to its essence, and then fractured and deconstructed, geometry becomes a language for narrative exploration. Whether it is to retire painting, as in the work of Saburo Murakami, or to reanimate it with new gestural vitality, as in the work of a new generation of artists, such as Elizabeth Murray, geometric painting and sculpture in the 1970s, which may be more psychological, metaphysical, or playful, becomes imbued with personal touch.

SABURO MURAKAMI
Sakuhin (*Work*), c. 1970
Synthetic-resin paint, canvas, cotton, board, and mixed media
85 ⅜ × 48 × 3 ½ in. (217 × 122 × 9 cm)
The Rachofsky Collection

JOEL SHAPIRO
Untitled (Bronze House), 1973–74
Bronze
6 × 5 × 4⅛ in. (15.2 × 12.7 × 10.5 cm)
Edition: 2 of 3
Collection of Robert and Marguerite Hoffman

ELIZABETH MURRAY
Small Town, 1980
Oil on canvas
Six parts, overall: 132 × 130 in. (335.3 × 330.2 cm)
The Rachofsky Collection

JACKIE WINSOR
Burnt Paper Piece, 1981-82
Wood, reams of paper, and hydrostone
32 ⅛ × 32 ⅛ × 32 ⅛ in. (81.6 × 81.6 × 81.6 cm)
Collection of Robert and Marguerite Hoffman

HEIDI BUCHER
Puerta Verde (Green Door), 1988
Gauze and caoutchouc skin
80 ¾ × 53 ⅞ in. (205 × 137 cm)
The Rose Collection

RICHARD FLEISCHNER
Square and Cylinder, 2009
Wax, wood, and paper
5 ¾ × 17 ½ × 7 ⅞ in. (14.6 × 44.4 × 20 cm)
Collection of Marguerite Steed Hoffman

GALLERY 10

In the face of an artistic language that had been reduced in a sense to nearly nothing, one of the biggest challenges to artists of the 1960s was to find valid and rigorous ways to work representation back into an artistic vocabulary that had essentially expunged it. (Pop achieved this, while maintaining the flatness of painting's surface, by appropriating the formats and means of representation of mass media.)

Even where representation remains, it tends to be infused with the language of geometry, as it is in Claes Oldenburg's triangles of pie, or obscured, as it is in Bruce Nauman's sculpture of what might appear to be simply a meandering line, which is, in fact, a cast of the contour of the artist's shoulder and arm. Geta Bratescu's softly geometric composition was formed, not in the spirit of pure abstraction, but with bits of worn fabric imbued with a presence of the lives with which they had been lived. Gordon Matta-Clark's quasi-nonobjective construction is a fragment cut from the walls of Food, both a functioning restaurant that he created in Soho and a living artwork. Paul McCarthy re-envisioned the simple act of drawing a line by hurling his own body through paint.

For so many artists, the grid becomes the validating structure through which the figure can reenter artistic discourse. This development is especially meaningful for women artists, traditionally trained in the male-dominated lineage of art history situated in the present by the language of geometric abstraction, itself an embodiment of authority; and culturally empowered by the women's movement. Indeed, the greatest force in shifting the paradigm from the abstraction of geometry to an examination of representation, identity, and the self was feminism. Before the rise of feminism, there was little place in mainstream contemporary art for narrative, intimacy, vulnerability, the small in scale, or content that was unabashedly personal. Voices that had previously been silenced or that had instinctively silenced themselves were beginning to break down many barriers.

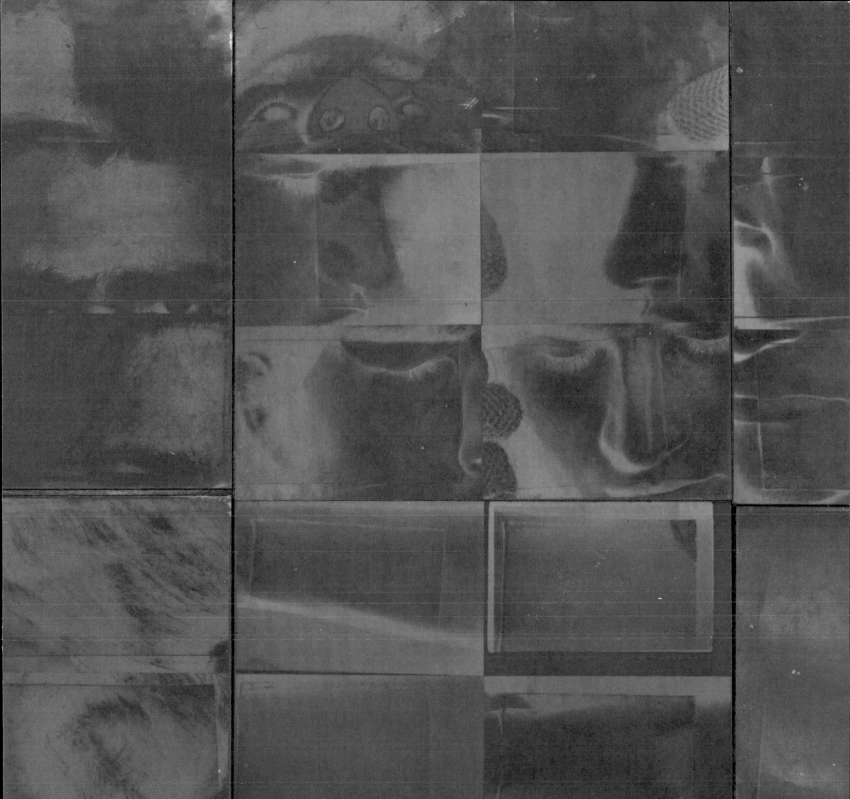

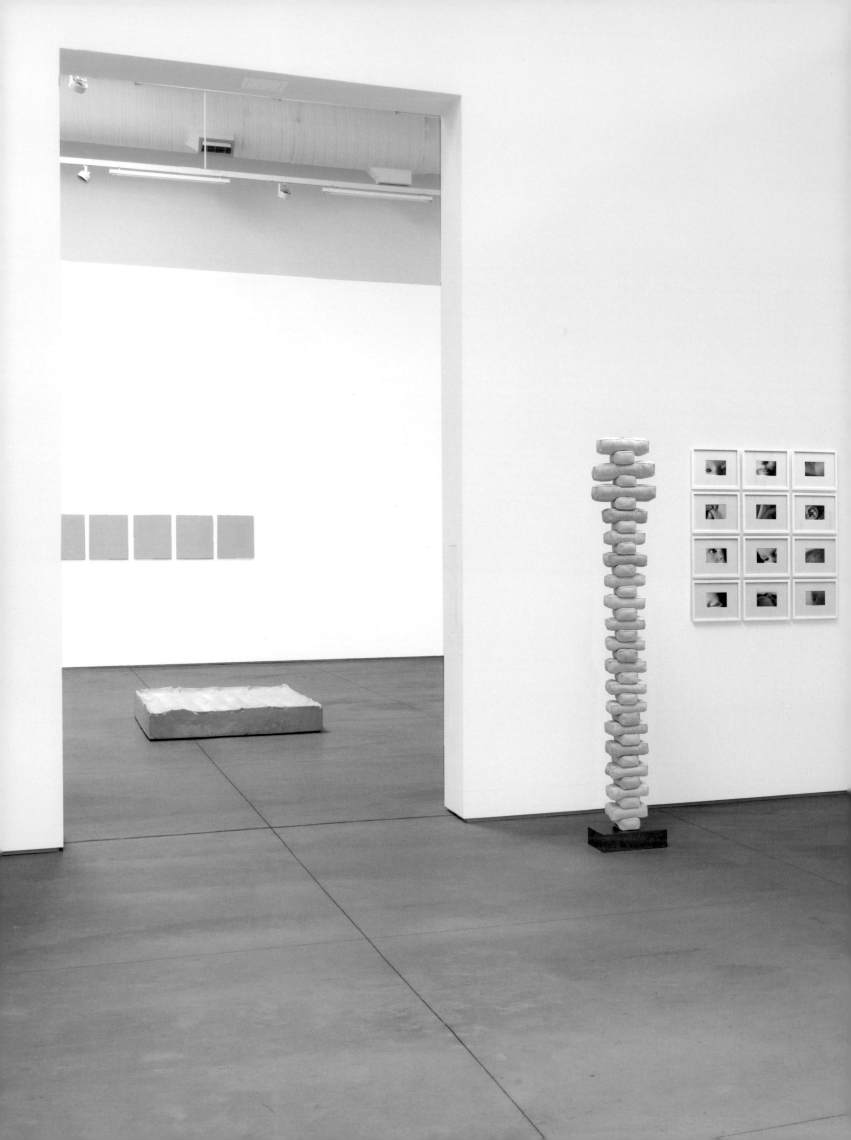

ria Woodhull while waiting for the paint to dry on

time; as Victoria Woodhull was the first woman to

the force of society came down upon her when she

seducing the married women of his parish. The

PAUL MCCARTHY
Face Painting—Floor, White Line, 1972 (printed 1989)
Gelatin silver prints
Two prints, each: 61 × 39 in. (154.9 × 99.1 cm)
Edition of 3 + 1 Artist's Proof
Sharon and Michael Young

GIUSEPPE PENONE
Svolgere la propria pelle (*To Unroll One's Skin*), 1970
Copper and wood
Four panels; top left, bottom left, and top right, each:
31 ½ × 55 ⅛ in. (80 × 140 cm); bottom right: 23 ⅝ × 55 ⅛ in. (60 × 140 cm)
The Rachofsky Collection

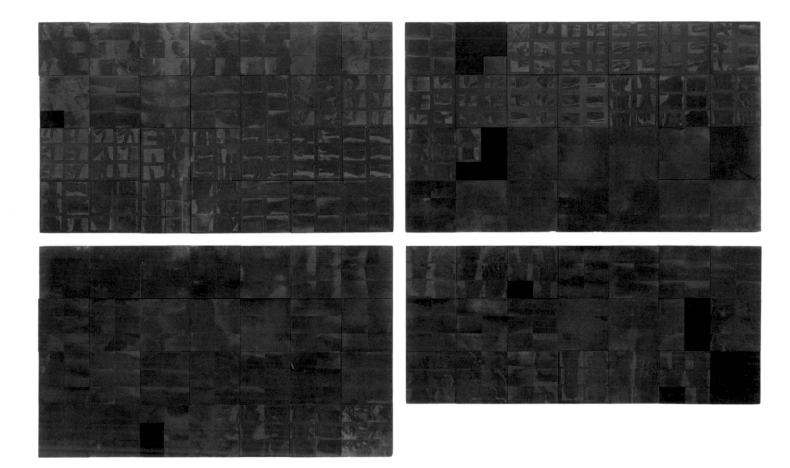

HANNAH WILKE
Untitled, 1975–78
Sixty ceramic sculptures and wooden board
Overall: 32 × 32 in. (81.3 × 81.3 cm)
Vitrine: 38 × 35 × 35 in. (96.5 × 88.9 × 88.9 cm)
Collection of Marguerite Steed Hoffman

JUDY CHICAGO
The Liberation of the Great Ladies, 1973
Sprayed acrylic and ink on canvas
40 × 40 in. (101.6 × 101.6 cm)
The Rachofsky Collection

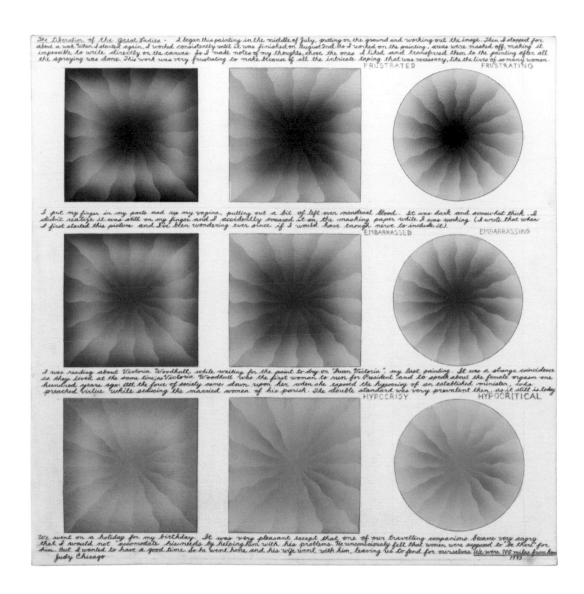

GARY HILL
Conundrum, 1995–98
Single-channel video installation, six monitors, custom casing,
switcher, laser disc player, and three laser discs
Edition: 5 of 6 + Artist's Proof
The Rachofsky Collection

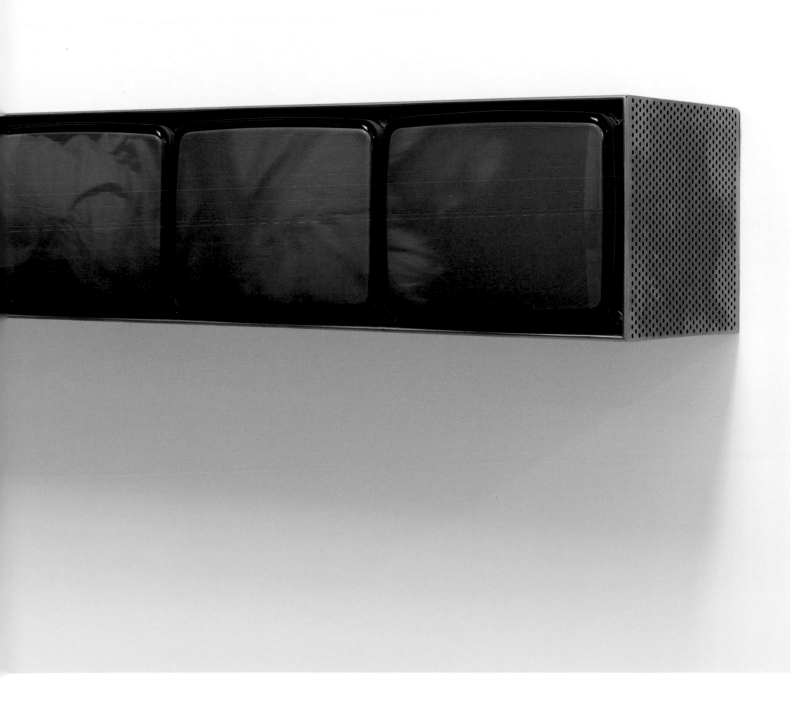

LOUISE BOURGEOIS
Untitled, 2002
Fabric and steel
76 × 12 × 10 in. (193 × 30.5 × 25.4 cm)
The Rose Collection

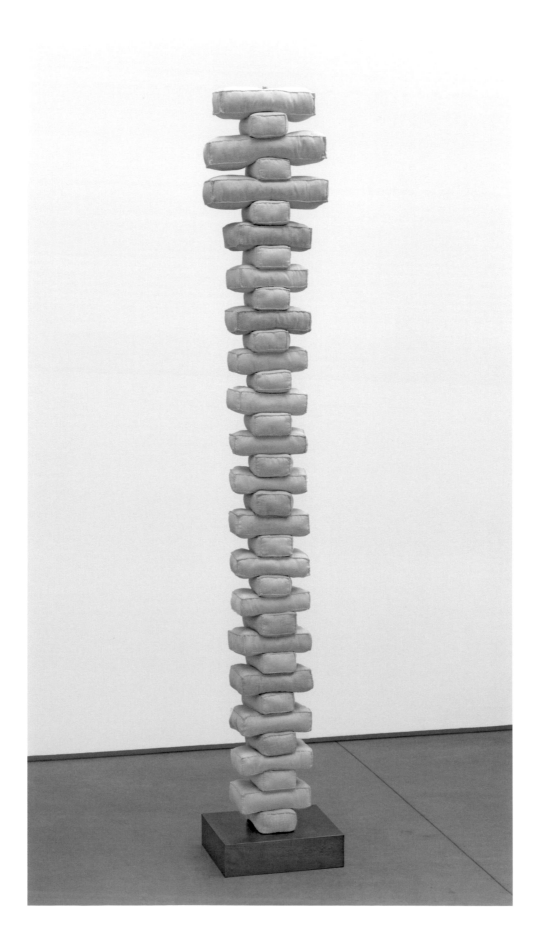

MARY KELLY
Primapara (Bathing Series), 1974
Black-and-white gelatin silver prints on fiber-base paper
Twelve prints, each: 8½ × 10½ in. (21.6 × 26.7 cm)
Edition: 3 of 3
The Rachofsky Collection

JOEL SHAPIRO
Untitled (Fingerprints), 1969–70
Ink on paper
17½ × 17½ in. (44.4 × 44.4 cm)
The Rose Collection

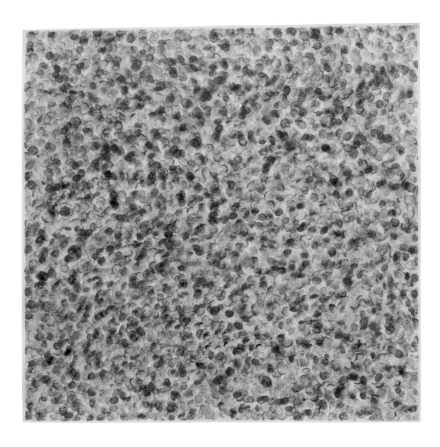

LOUISE BOURGEOIS
Torso, 1996
Fabric
12 × 25 ½ × 16 ½ in. (30.5 × 64.8 × 41.9 cm)
Collection of Robert and Marguerite Hoffman

GORDON MATTA-CLARK
Untitled (Food, Prince St. at Wooster St. NY), 1973
Wall fragment: wood, nails, metal, and pencil
19½ × 18⅜ × 4 in. (49.5 × 46.7 × 10.2 cm)
The Rose Collection

GIUSEPPE PENONE
Albero di 5 metri (*Tree of 5 Meters*), 1969
Wood
196 ⅞ × 11 ¾ × 5 ⅞ in. (500 × 30 × 15 cm)
The Rose Collection

CLAES OLDENBURG
Four Pies in a Glass Case, 1961
Muslin soaked in plaster over chicken wire,
painted with enamel; glass case
5 ½ × 30 × 9 in. (13.3 × 76.2 × 22.9 cm)
Collection of Robert and Marguerite Hoffman

BRUCE NAUMAN
Untitled, 1965
Fiberglass and polyester resin
67 ¼ × 6 ¼ × 3 ⅛ in. (170.8 × 15.9 × 7.9 cm)
The Rose Collection

GALLERY 11

Charles Ray, an artist at the forefront of the generation that would come into its own in the 1980s, made this work as a student. He takes on the geometric language of modern sculpture, rendering its once-muscular components here tenuously interdependent, creating a portrait of their impending collapse.

CHARLES RAY
One-Stop Gallery, Iowa City, Iowa, 1971/1998
Concrete blocks and painted steel
Overall: 30 × 30 ft. (9.1 × 9.1 m)
Dallas Museum of Art, DMA/amfAR Benefit Auction Fund and the
Contemporary Art Fund: Gift of Mr. and Mrs. Vernon E. Faulconer,
Mr. and Mrs. Bryant M. Hanley Jr., Marguerite and Robert K. Hoffman,
Cindy and Howard Rachofsky, Deedie and Rusty Rose, Gayle and
Paul Stoffel, and two anonymous donors

GALLERY 12

For artists whose voices reach momentum in the 1980s, art becomes unmistakably representational. Now the order is reversed: content determines form, and content is decidedly psychological, whether the focus is personal or cultural. Nonetheless, subtly or overtly, geometry remains as a significant underlying stratum in a new era of the artistic exploration of the self.

Charles Ray's *Rotating Circle*, 1988 (p. 288), might at first seem to be pure abstraction, but its dimensions—almost those of a human face—and its installation—intentionally at the artist's own height—give the work the presence of a surrogate self-portrait, and it becomes nothing less than a portrayal of psychological turbulence. If Irwin's circular disk is about the limitlessness of perception, Ray's rotating circle, spinning so fast that we cannot see it move, suggests a limit beyond our ability to perceive it. Félix González-Torres's graph paintings recall the poetic gentleness of Agnes Martin's paintings, but here, what seems to be abstraction is in fact the charting of the deterioration of a man dying from AIDS, portraying mortality with a universal language. The syntax of abstraction takes on new meaning in a new era in which specific content is found where pure abstraction once reigned.

In the work of Christopher Wool, lines become the stenciled letters of language, articulating both the word they spell and the identity it conjures. In the work of Annette Messager, the grid is fragmented into a more aggressively psychological portrayal of the self, and it is similarly employed in the work of Martin Kippenberger to depict the machinery of culture. Work that is even more emphatically representational, such as Robert Gober's sculptures of sinks and doors, while deeply personal in meaning, still possesses an underlying geometric order informed by the rigors of Minimalism.

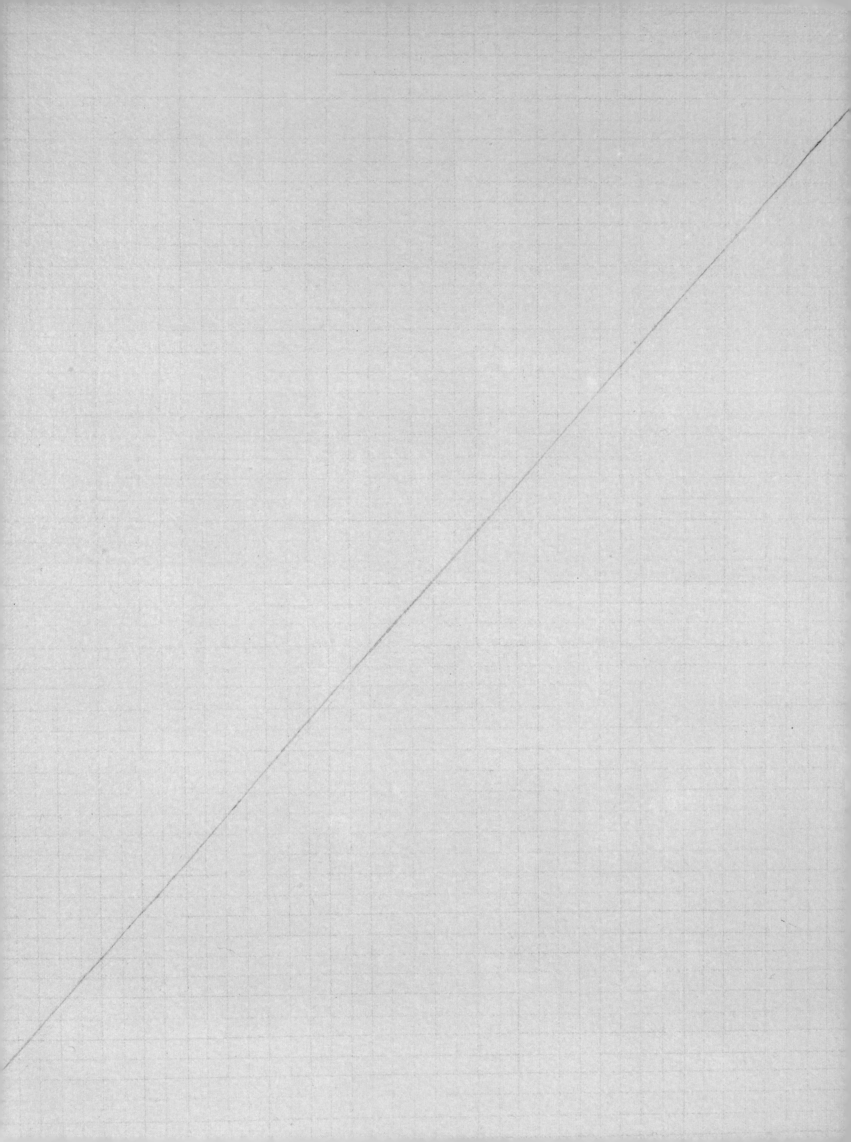

DAVID WATKINS
Necklace, 1977
Gold
7 ¼ × 8 ¼ × ¾ in. (18.4 × 21 × 1.9 cm)
Dallas Museum of Art, gift of Edward W. and Deedie Potter Rose,
formerly Inge Asenbaum Collection, Gallery Am Graben in Vienna

ROBERT GOBER
Untitled, 1985
Plaster, wire lath, wood, steel, and semigloss enamel paint
14 × 24 × 19 in. (35.6 × 61 × 48.3 cm)
Collection of Robert and Marguerite Hoffman

FÉLIX GONZÁLEZ-TORRES
"Untitled" (Perfect Lovers), 1987–90
Wall clocks
Two parts, each: 13 ½ in. diameter
Overall: 13 ½ × 27 × 1 ¼ in. (34.3 × 68.6 × 3.2 cm)
Edition of 3, 1 Artist's Proof
Dallas Museum of Art, fractional gift of The Rachofsky Collection

FÉLIX GONZÁLEZ-TORRES
"Untitled" (7 Days of Bloodworks), 1988
Gesso, acrylic, and graphite on canvas
Seven parts, each: 20 × 16 in. (50.8 × 40.6 cm)
Overall dimensions vary with installation
The Rachofsky Collection

CHARLES RAY
Rotating Circle, 1988
Electric motor with disc
Diameter: 9 in. (22.9 cm)
Dallas Museum of Art, fractional gift of The Rachofsky Collection

ANNETTE MESSAGER
Mes voeux (My Vows), 1989
Acrylic on black-and-white photographs under glass and string
78 ¾ × 55 in. (200 × 139.7 cm)
The Rachofsky Collection

ROBERT GOBER
Two Doors, 1989
Wood and enamel paint
Each: 84 × 31 × 1½ in. (213.4 × 78.7 × 3.8 cm)
Overall: 84 × 73 × 1½ in. (213.4 × 185.4 × 3.8 cm)
Collection of Marguerite Steed Hoffman

CHRISTOPHER WOOL
Untitled, 1990
Enamel and acrylic on aluminum
96 × 64 in. (243.8 × 162.6 cm)
Collection of Marguerite Steed Hoffman

RACHEL WHITEREAD
Untitled (Air Bed), 1992
Plastic and polystyrene
8⅝ × 47¼ × 76⅜ in. (21.9 × 120 × 194 cm)
Collection of Robert and Marguerite Hoffman

LEONILSON
Auto-retrato (Self-portrait), 1993
Steel, fabric, sewing, and embroidery
4 × 4 × 4 in. (10.2 × 10.2 × 10.2 cm)
The Rose Collection

ROBERT GOBER
Untitled, 2003–2005
Bronze and oil paint
9 × 46½ × 61 in. (22.9 × 118.1 × 154.9 cm)
The Rose Collection and The Rachofsky Collection

GALLERIES 13, 14, AND 15

For other artists who emerge in the 1980s, and successive generations, geometry offers a maximalist field in which to explore a wide range of artistic concerns. Even in work that veers toward abstraction, there is often an underlying sense of representation and psychological content. Jim Hodges's shaped mirrored panels, each reflecting in the other, form a psychological space that also engages the viewer. Mona Hatoum's blade, which is simultaneously scoring and erasing a circle of sand, suggests the fugitive nature of time and existence. Sherrie Levine's monochrome panels, each a computer-generated contraction of all the colors in a painting by Piet Mondrian, telescope, in a multiple instant, the history of painting from modernism to Minimalism. Gabriel Orozco's circled broken wall fragments suggest a crumbling of culture. Luc Tuymans's *Slide #1*, 2002 (p. 334), is a portrayal of a notion of picture making. All we are shown is a rectangle of light, light being a universal symbol of creative inspiration and of life, in this case tinged with a somewhat melancholic aura of life unseen. Donald Moffett uses the simple geometric language of abstraction as a coded implication of sexual identity.

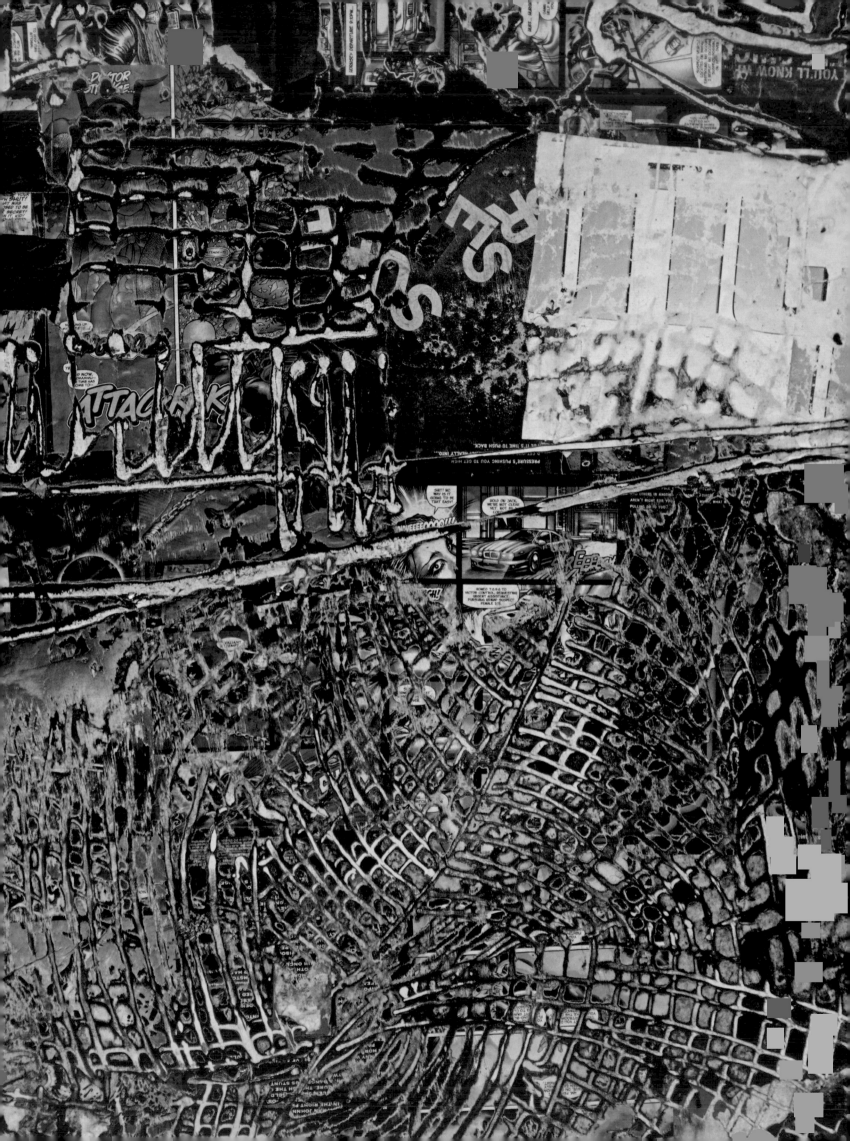

JORGE MACCHI
And, 2006
Newspaper cutting, pinned on paper
59⅜ × 79½ × 8¼ in. (150.9 × 201.9 × 20.8 cm)
The Rose Collection

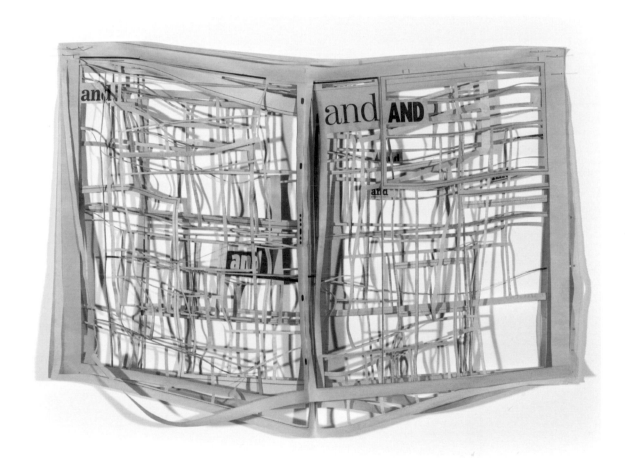

RICHARD PRINCE
Untitled (Check Painting), 2006
Acrylic and checks on canvas
108 × 156 in. (274.3 × 396.2 cm)
Collection of Marguerite Steed Hoffman

TOM FRIEDMAN
Untitled (dots connected by lines and arrows), 1997
Ink on paper
54 × 42½ in. (137.2 × 108 cm)
The Rose Collection

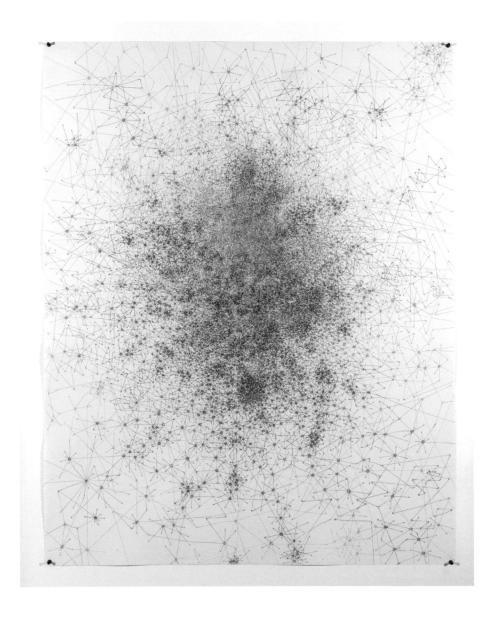

GIOVANNI CORVAJA
Brooch, 1999
950 platinum, 18 karat gold, and fine gold
2 ½ × 2 ½ in. (6.5 x 6.5 cm)
The Rose Collection

ANNETTE LAWRENCE
Moons, 1995–96
Mixed media on paper
Thirteen panels, unframed, each: 15 × 10 in. (38.1 × 25.4 cm)
Overall, framed: 78 ¾ × 58 ¾ in. (200 × 149.2 cm)
The Rachofsky Collection

TOM FRIEDMAN
Untitled, 1990
Toilet paper
14 × 14 × 4 ½ in. (35.6 × 35.6 × 11.4 cm)
Collection of Marguerite Steed Hoffman

JIM HODGES
Toward Great Becoming (blue/blue), 2014
Mirror on panel
Left panel: 57 ⅞ × 38 ⅜ in. (147 × 97.5 cm);
Right panel: 60 × 30 ½ in. (152.4 × 77.5 cm)
Amy and Vernon Faulconer and The Rachofsky Collection

MONA HATOUM
+ and -, 1994
Hardwood, steel blades, electric motor, and sand
3 × 11 ½ × 11 ½ in. (7.6 × 29.2 × 29.2 cm)
Edition: 9 of 14
The Rachofsky Collection

EDWARD KRASINSKI
Intervention, 1991
Mixed media and blue Scotch tape
39 ⅜ × 51 ⅛ × 5 ⅝ in. (100 × 129.9 × 14.3 cm)
The Rachofsky Collection

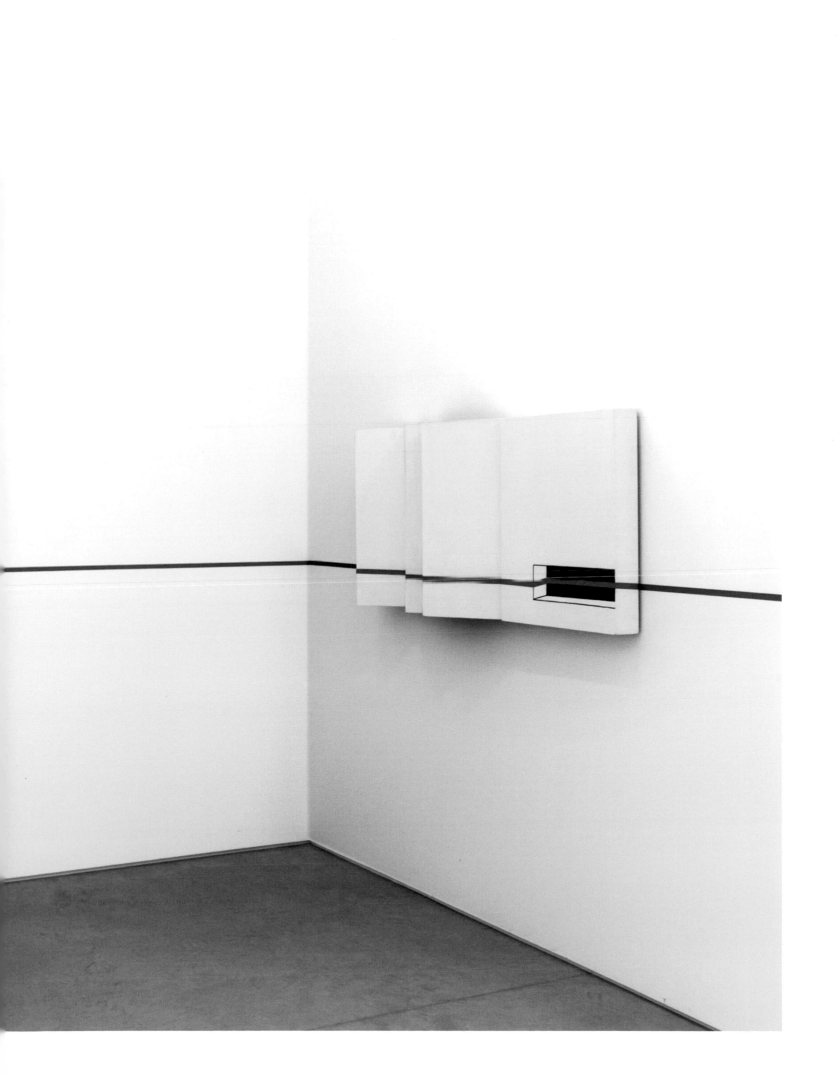

FERNANDA GOMES
Untitled, 2011
Wood and paint
13 ¼ × 24 ½ × 1 ½ in. (33.7 × 62.2 × 3.8 cm)
The Rose Collection

FERNANDA GOMES
Untitled, 2012
Cardboard
22 ¼ × 11 × 2 in. (56.5 × 27.9 × 5.1 cm)
The Rose Collection

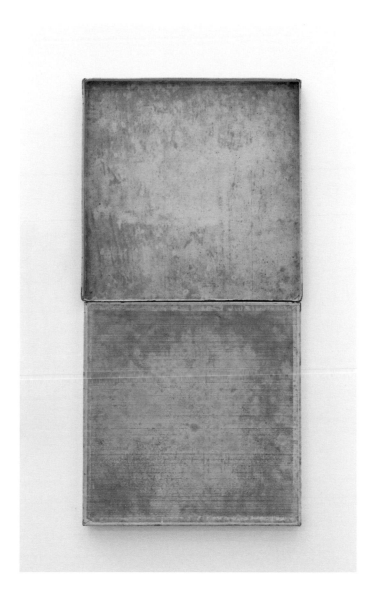

MARK BRADFORD
A Truly Rich Man is One Whose Children Run Into His Arms When
His Hands are Empty, 2008
Mixed media collage on canvas
102 × 144 in. (259.1 × 365.8 cm)
Collection of Marguerite Steed Hoffman

IRAN DO ESPÍRITO SANTO
Restless 23, 2004
Sandblasted glass and mirror
20 × 89 in. (50.8 × 226.1 cm)
The Rachofsky Collection

PAUL SIETSEMA
Painter's Mussel 6, 2011
Ink on paper in artist's frame
72 ¼ × 71 ¼ in. (183.5 × 181 cm)
The Rachofsky Collection

MATT JOHNSON
Dice, 2010
Cut meteorite
Two parts, each: approximately 1 × 1 × 1 in. (2.5 × 2.5 × 2.5 cm)
Edition: 1 of 3
The Rose Collection

DONALD MOFFETT
Lot 031507 (Oolo), 2007
Oil, rayon, plated nickel, rabbit-skin glue, and polyvinyl acetate on linen
in artist's painted wood frame
31 ½ × 27 ½ in. (80 × 69.8 cm)
The Rachofsky Collection

GABRIEL OROZCO
Inner Circles of the Wall, 1999
Plaster and graphite
Installation width: approximately 35 ft. (10.7 m)
The Rachofsky Collection, Collection of Deedie and Rusty Rose, and
Dallas Museum of Art through the DMA/amfAR Benefit Auction Fund

MANFRED PERNICE
Untitled (two cubes), 2008
MDF and paint
Two parts, each: 19 ¾ × 19 ¾ × 19 ¾ in. (50.2 × 50.2 × 50.2 cm)
The Rose Collection

DAMIÁN ORTEGA
Tortillas Construction Module, 1998
Corn tortillas
Installation dimensions variable
The Rose Collection

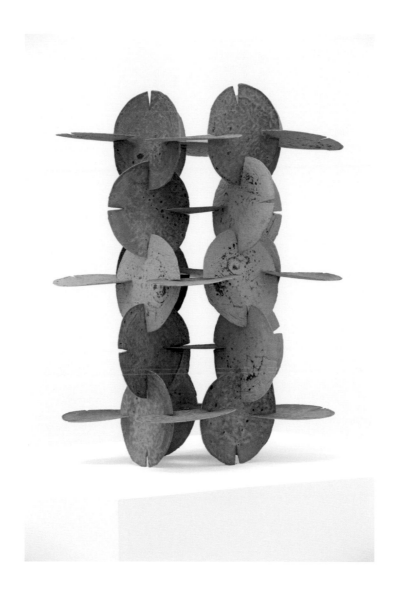

GALLERY 16

The range of possibility for artists today is broader and more pluralistic than it has been in recent decades—representation, abstraction, gestural surfaces or processed ones, sculptural works that refer to painting and paintings that have sculptural presence, all are feasibly valid, at least for now. And yet, the language of geometry still remains a structural syntax for so much art making, both abstract and representational. Mark Grotjahn brings new relevance to abstract painting, a lineage that might otherwise have seemed fully played out. Donald Judd's material and structural logic is alive and well in the image-driven work of R. H. Quaytman, and Barnett Newman's zip is reconsidered from both an architectural and sculptural perspective in the work of Nate Lowman. The rigor of the reductivism that concluded with Minimalism, and the ensuing rebellion against it, have made all this possibility possible.

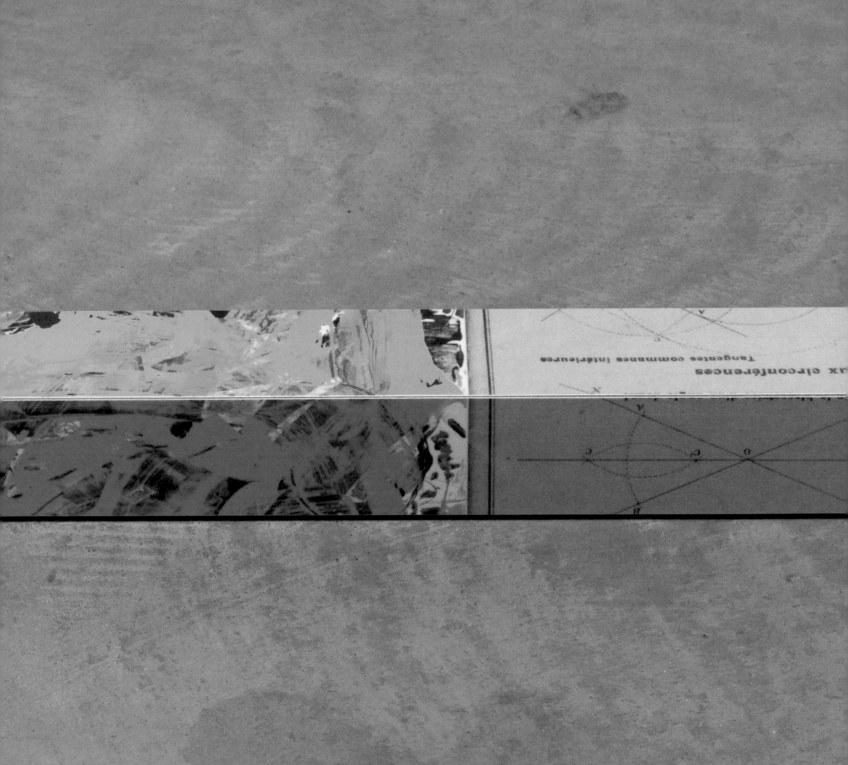

NATE LOWMAN
Broken Zip, 2010
Metal
Approximately 180 × 3 × 5 in. (457.2 × 7.6 × 12.7 cm)
Installation dimensions variable
The Rachofsky Collection

WADE GUYTON
Untitled, 2006
Inkjet on linen
89 ⅜ × 54 ¼ × 1 ⅜ in. (227 × 137.8 × 3.5 cm)
The Rachofsky Collection

JIM LAMBIE
The Doors (Morrison Hotel), 2005
Wooden doors, mirrors, and gloss paint
80¾ × 75⅞ × 19½ in. (203.8 × 192.7 × 49.5 cm)
The Rachofsky Collection and the Dallas Museum of Art
through the DMA/amfAR Benefit Auction Fund

JEPPE HEIN
Inside Cube, 2008
Powder-coated aluminum
2 × 2 × 2 in. (5.1 × 5.1 × 5.1 cm)
Edition: 1 of 3
The Rachofsky Collection

R. H. QUAYTMAN
Passing Through the Opposite of What It Approaches, Chapter 25
(after James Coleman's slide piece), 2012
Oil, tempera, silkscreen ink, and gesso on wood
Three parts—large: 37 × 60 in. (94.1 × 152.4 cm); small: 12 ⅜ × 20 in. (31.4 × 50.8 cm);
shelf: 3 × 59 ½ × 1 ½ in. (7.6 × 151.1 × 3.8 cm)
The Rachofsky Collection

MARK GROTJAHN
Untitled (Blue Butterfly Light to Dark XI 661), 2006
Oil on linen
77 × 54 in. (195.6 × 137.2 cm)
The Rachofsky Collection

MESCHAC GABA
Benin Maison Private (Architectural wig), 2008
Braided wig of synthetic hair
24 × 9½ × 9½ in. (61 × 24.1 × 24.1 cm)
The Rose Collection

FRANCES STARK
The world becomes a private world and shines like a rainbow, 1998
Carbon, oil, and permanent marker on paper
87 × 60 in. (221 × 152.4 cm)
The Rachofsky Collection

LUISA LAMBRI
Untitled (Strathmore Apartments, #46), 2002
Laserchrome print
43 ¼ × 51 ⅜ in. (110 × 130 cm)
Edition: 1 of 5 + Artist's Proof
The Rachofsky Collection

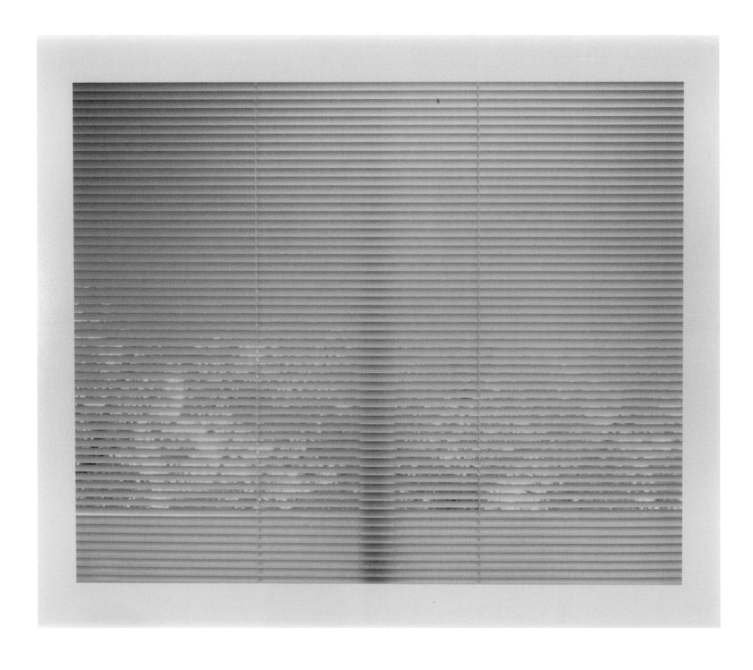

ALEXANDRE DA CUNHA
Arcadia, 2007
Cleaning mop head, bathroom mat, wool, tapestry canvas,
and wooden stretcher
72 ½ × 53 ½ in. (184 × 136 cm)
The Rose Collection

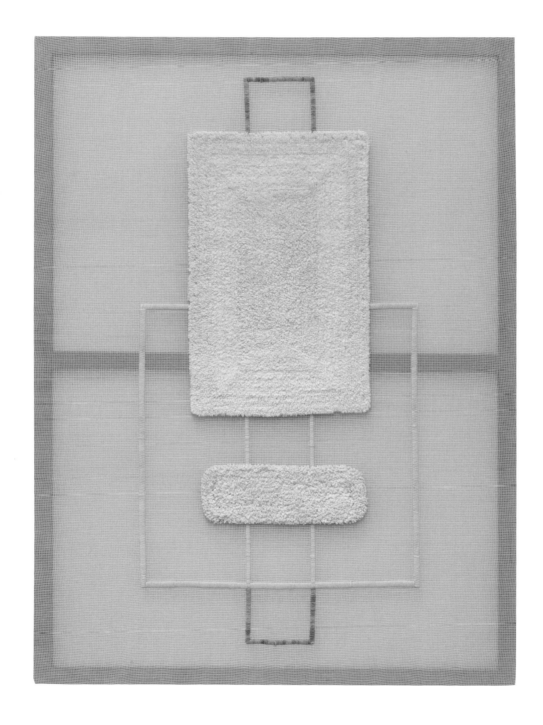

CHEYNEY THOMPSON
Pedestal (P), 2012
MDF and HPL
2 in. × 33 ft. 3 in. × 2 in. (5.1 cm × 10.1 m × 5.1 cm)
The Rachofsky Collection

JOSEF ALBERS
Homage to the Square (732), 1961
Oil on Masonite
Panel: 30⅛ × 30⅛ in. (76.5 × 76.5 cm)
Framed: 30⅝ × 30⅝ × 1¼ in.
(77.8 × 77.8 × 3.2 cm)
Dallas Museum of Art, gift of Anni Albers
and the Josef Albers Foundation, Inc.
Page 102; detail, page i

PETER ALEXANDER
Pink Green Cube, 1967
Cast polyester resin
8 × 8 × 8 in. (20.3 × 20.3 × 20.3 cm)
Pedestal: 45 × 14 × 14 in.
(114.3 × 35.6 × 35.6 cm)
The Rose Collection
Page 192

GIOVANNI ANSELMO
Senza titolo (Untitled), 1967
Wood, water, and Formica
63 × 23⅝ × 23⅝ in. (160 × 60 × 60 cm)
The Rachofsky Collection
Page 68

RICHARD ARTSCHWAGER
Swivel, 1964
Formica on wood
53⅜ × 25½ × 30¾ in.
(135.6 × 64.8 × 78.1 cm)
The Rose Collection and
The Rachofsky Collection
Page 155

ALIGHIERO BOETTI
Zig Zag, 1966
Fabric and aluminum
19⅝ × 19⅝ × 19⅝ in. (49.8 × 49.8 × 49.8 cm)
The Rose Collection
Page 127; detail, page 380

LOUISE BOURGEOIS
Torso, 1996
Fabric
12 × 25½ × 16½ in. (30.5 × 64.8 × 41.9 cm)
Collection of Robert and Marguerite Hoffman
Page 253

Untitled, 2002
Fabric and steel
76 × 12 × 10 in. (193 × 30.5 × 25.4 cm)
The Rose Collection
Page 248

MARK BRADFORD
*A Truly Rich Man is One Whose Children
Run Into His Arms When His Hands
are Empty*, 2008
Mixed media collage on canvas
102 × 144 in. (259.1 × 365.8 cm)
Collection of Marguerite Steed Hoffman
Pages 328–29; detail, page 310

GETA BRATESCU
Vestigii No. 4 (Vestiges No. 4), 1978
Textile collage on paper
Framed: 13⅝ × 19⅝ in. (34.6 × 49.8 cm)
The Rose Collection
Page 256

MARCEL BROODTHAERS
*Ovale d'oeufs 1234567 (Oval of
eggs 1234567)*, 1965
Eggshells and oil paint on wood panel
39⅜ × 31½ × 4¾ in. (100 × 80 × 12.1 cm)
Dallas Museum of Art, fractional gift of
The Rachofsky Collection
Page 189; detail, page 375

HEIDI BUCHER
Puerta Verde (Green Door), 1988
Gauze and caoutchouc skin
80¾ × 53⅞ in. (205 × 137 cm)
The Rose Collection
Page 219

ALBERTO BURRI
Cretto B2, 1973
Acrovinyl on cellotex
59 × 49¼ in. (149.9 × 125.1 cm)
The Rachofsky Collection
Page 195

JAMES LEE BYARS
Is, 1989
Gilded marble
Diameter: 23½ in. (59.7 cm)
Collection of Marguerite Steed Hoffman
Page 198

SERGIO CAMARGO
Relief No. 262, 1969
Wood relief and paint
Panel: 47¼ × 39⅜ × 3⅛ in.
(120 × 100 × 7.9 cm)
Dallas Museum of Art,
gift of Mr. and Mrs. James H. Clark
Page 194; detail, page iv

#56 Prototype of Port Bacarés Sculpture, 1964
Painted wood
26 × 8⅛ × 8½ in. (66 × 20.6 × 21.6 cm)
The Rose Collection
Page 106

ENRICO CASTELLANI
Superficie Blu (Blue Surface), 1965
Oil on canvas
72 × 107¾ in. (182.9 × 273.7 cm)
The Rachofsky Collection
Pages 190–91

JOHN CHAMBERLAIN
Rap Psalm II, 1999
Painted chromium and painted steel
103½ × 59 × 47 in.
(262.9 × 149.9 × 119.4 cm)
The Rachofsky Collection
Page 170; detail, page v

JUDY CHICAGO
The Liberation of the Great Ladies, 1973
Sprayed acrylic and ink on canvas
40 × 40 in. (101.6 × 101.6 cm)
The Rachofsky Collection
Page 245; detail, page 238

LYGIA CLARK
Casulo (Cocoon), 1959
Acrylic paint, balsam, and graphite
5¼ × 5¼ in. (13.3 × 13.3 cm)
The Rose Collection
Page 152

Bicho—Em si (Creature—In Itself), 1962
Aluminum
12¼ × 9⅞ × 8⅝ in. (31.1 × 25.1 × 21.9 cm)
Installation dimensions variable
The Rose Collection
Page 153

*Estruturas de caixa de fósforos
(Matchbox Structures)*, 1964
Gouache paint, matchboxes, and glue
3⅛ × 5½ × 2 in. (7.9 × 14 × 5.1 cm)
The Rose Collection
Page 154

TONY CONRAD
Yellow Movie 2/26/73, 1973
Emulsion: Empire Yellow Gloss Enamel
by Eaglo, odorless Magicote
Base: White canvas, stretched
Screen: 24 × 33 in. (61 × 83.8 cm)
Overall: 33 × 42 in. (83.8 × 106.7 cm)
The Rose Collection
Page 76

GIOVANNI CORVAJA
Brooch, 1999
950 platinum, 18 karat gold, and fine gold
2½ × 2½ in. (6.5 × 6.5 cm)
The Rose Collection
Page 317

ALEXANDRE DA CUNHA
Arcadia, 2007
Cleaning mop head, bathroom mat, wool,
tapestry canvas, and wooden stretcher
72½ × 53½ in. (184 × 136 cm)
The Rose Collection
Page 363; detail, page 343

DADAMAINO
*Volume a modulazioni sfasate
(Volume of Displaced Modules)*, 1960
Sheets of plastic applied on
superimposed frames
15¾ × 11¾ in. (40 × 30 cm)
The Rose Collection
Page 185; detail, page 182

DAN FLAVIN
*alternate diagonals of March 2, 1964
(to Don Judd)*, March 2, 1964
Daylight and cool white fluorescent tubing
Overall: 144 × 12 in. (365.8 × 30.5 cm)
Dallas Museum of Art, gift of Janie C. Lee
Page 41

RICHARD FLEISCHNER
Square and Cylinder, 2009
Wax, wood, and paper
5¾ × 17½ × 7⅞ in. (14.6 × 44.4 × 20 cm)
Collection of Marguerite Steed Hoffman
Page 223

LUCIO FONTANA
*Concetto spaziale, Attesa (Spatial
Concept, Expectation)*, 1964
Waterpaint on canvas
45⅝ × 31⅞ in. (115.9 × 81 cm)
The Rachofsky Collection
Page 125

*Concetto spaziale, la fine di Dio
(Spatial Concept, The End of God)*, 1964
Oil on canvas
70 × 48½ in. (177.8 × 123.2 cm)
The Rachofsky Collection
Page 188; detail, page iii

TOM FRIEDMAN
Untitled, 1990
Toilet paper
14 × 14 × 4½ in. (35.6 × 35.6 × 11.4 cm)
Collection of Marguerite Steed Hoffman
Page 319

*Untitled (dots connected by
lines and arrows)*, 1997
Ink on paper
54 × 42½ in. (137.2 × 108 cm)
The Rose Collection
Page 316

MESCHAC GABA
Benin Maison Private (Architectural wig), 2008
Braided wig of synthetic hair
24 × 9½ × 9½ in. (61 × 24.1 × 24.1 cm)
The Rose Collection
Page 360

GILBERT & GEORGE
Prostitute Poof, 1977
Mixed media
95 × 79 in. (241.3 × 200.7 cm)
The Rachofsky Collection
Page 250

ROBERT GOBER
Untitled, 1985
Plaster, wire lath, wood, steel, and semigloss
enamel paint
14 × 24 × 19 in. (35.6 × 61 × 48.3 cm)
Collection of Robert and Marguerite Hoffman
Page 283

Two Doors, 1989
Wood and enamel paint
Each: 84 × 31 × 1½ in.
(213.4 × 78.7 × 3.8 cm)
Overall: 84 × 73 × 1½ in.
(213.4 × 185.4 × 3.8 cm)
Collection of Marguerite Steed Hoffman
Page 290

Untitled, 2003–2005
Bronze and oil paint
9 × 46½ × 61 in. (22.9 × 118.1 × 154.9 cm)
The Rose Collection and
The Rachofsky Collection
Page 295; detail, page 271

FERNANDA GOMES
Untitled, 2011
Wood and paint
13 ¼ × 24 ½ × 1 ½ in. (33.7 × 62.2 × 3.8 cm)
The Rose Collection
Page 326

Untitled, 2012
Cardboard
22 ¼ × 11 × 2 in. (56.5 × 27.9 × 5.1 cm)
The Rose Collection
Page 327

FÉLIX GONZÁLEZ-TORRES
"Untitled" (Perfect Lovers), 1987–90
Wall clocks
Two parts, each: 13 ½ in. diameter
Overall: 13 ½ × 27 × 1 ¼ in.
(34.3 × 68.6 × 3.2 cm)
Edition of 3, 1 Artist's Proof
Dallas Museum of Art, fractional gift
of The Rachofsky Collection
Page 286

"Untitled" (7 Days of Bloodworks), 1988
Gesso, acrylic, and graphite on canvas
Seven parts, each: 20 × 16 in. (50.8 × 40.6 cm)
Overall dimensions vary with installation
The Rachofsky Collection
Page 287; detail, page 278

VICTOR GRIPPO
Sin título (Untitled), 1965
Oil on canvas
35 ½ × 19 ¾ in. (90.2 × 50.2 cm)
The Rose Collection
Page 126

Vida, Muerte, Resurrección (Life, Death, Resurrection), 1980
Five hollow geometrical lead bodies;
five hollow geometrical lead bodies filled
with black and red beans; water; glass box
Overall: 19 ½ × 47 ½ × 31 ½ in.
(49.5 × 120.6 × 80 cm)
The Rose Collection
Page 169; detail, page 146

MARK GROTJAHN
Untitled (Blue Butterfly Light to Dark XI 661),
2006
Oil on linen
77 × 54 in. (195.6 × 137.2 cm)
The Rachofsky Collection
Page 359

WADE GUYTON
Untitled, 2006
Inkjet on linen
89 ⅜ × 54 ¼ × 1 ⅜ in. (227 × 137.8 × 3.5 cm)
The Rachofsky Collection
Page 354

MONA HATOUM
+ and –, 1994
Hardwood, steel blades, electric motor, and sand
3 × 11 ½ × 11 ½ in. (7.6 × 29.2 × 29.2 cm)
Edition: 9 of 14
The Rachofsky Collection
Page 321

MARY HEILMANN
August, 2004
Oil on canvas
40 × 32 in. (101.6 × 81.3 cm)
Amy and Vernon Faulconer
Page 222

JEPPE HEIN
Inside Cube, 2008
Powder-coated aluminum
2 × 2 × 2 in. (5.1 × 5.1 × 5.1 cm)
Edition: 1 of 3
The Rachofsky Collection
Page 356

MICHAEL HEIZER
Untitled #2, 1975
Polyvinyl, latex, and aluminum
powder on canvas
Diameter: 96 in. (243.8 cm)
The Rose Collection
Page 77

GARY HILL
Conundrum, 1995–98
Single-channel video installation, six
monitors, custom casing, switcher, laser
disc player, and three laser discs
Edition: 5 of 6 + Artist's Proof
The Rachofsky Collection
Pages 246–47

JIM HODGES
Toward Great Becoming (blue/blue), 2014
Mirror on panel
Left panel: 57 ⅞ × 38 ⅜ in. (147 × 97.5 cm)
Right panel: 60 × 30 ½ in. (152.4 × 77.5 cm)
Amy and Vernon Faulconer and
The Rachofsky Collection
Page 320

NORIO IMAI
White Ceremony/Toward #1, 1966–70
Acrylic, cotton cloth, and plastic pattern
28 ½ × 15 ½ × 3 ⅛ in. (72.5 × 39.5 × 8 cm)
The Rachofsky Collection
Page 128; detail, page ii

ROBERT IRWIN
Untitled, 1968–69
Acrylic lacquer on formed acrylic plastic
Diameter: 54 in. (137.2 cm)
Dallas Museum of Art, fractional gift
of The Rachofsky Collection
Page 193

Little Jazz, 2010
Light + Shadow + Reflection + Color
72 × 81 ⅜ × 4 ⅝ in. (182.9 × 206.7 × 11.7 cm)
Amy and Vernon Faulconer and
The Rachofsky Collection
Page 79

SERGEJ JENSEN
Untitled (Ohne Titel), 2001
Gouache and oil crayon on linen
70 ⅞ × 63 in. (180 × 160 cm)
The Rachofsky Collection
Page 364

MATT JOHNSON
Dice, 2010
Cut meteorite
Two parts, each: approximately 1 × 1 × 1 in.
(2.5 × 2.5 × 2.5 cm)
Edition: 1 of 3
The Rose Collection
Page 333

DONALD JUDD
Untitled, 1965
Galvanized iron and brown enamel
on aluminum
30 × 150 × 30 in. (76.2 × 381 × 76.2 cm)
Collection of Robert and Marguerite Hoffman
Page 42

Untitled, 1965
Stainless steel with fluorescent plexiglass
20 × 48 × 34 in. (50.8 × 121.9 × 86.4 cm)
The Rachofsky Collection
Page 43

Untitled, 1970
Clear and purple anodized aluminum
Overall: 8 ¼ × 253 ⅜ × 8 ¼ in.
(21 × 643.6 × 21 cm)
Dallas Museum of Art, fractional gift
of The Rachofsky Collection
Pages 48–49

ELLSWORTH KELLY
Sanary, 1952
Oil on wood
51 ½ × 60 in. (130.8 × 152.4 cm)
Collection of Robert and Marguerite Hoffman
Page 33

Black and White, 1967
Oil on canvas, two joined panels
82 × 144 in. (208.3 × 365.8 cm)
Collection of Robert and Marguerite Hoffman
Page 46

Two Grays I, 1975
Oil on canvas, two joined panels
92 × 102 in. (233.7 × 259.1 cm)
Collection of Robert and Marguerite Hoffman
Page 50

MARY KELLY
Primapara (Bathing Series), 1974
Black-and-white gelatin silver prints
on fiber-base paper
Twelve prints, each: 8 ½ × 10 ½ in.
(21.6 × 26.7 cm)
Edition: 3 of 3
The Rachofsky Collection
Page 249

MARTIN KIPPENBERGER
11.-13. Preis (aus der Serie Preis-Bilder)
[*11.-13. Prize (from the series Prize/Price
Pictures)*], 1987
Oil on canvas
59 × 96 ½ in. (150 × 245 cm)
Amy and Vernon Faulconer
Pages 284–85

YVES KLEIN
Untitled Monogold, 1961
Gold leaf on panel
24 ⅜ × 17 ¾ in. (62 × 45 cm)
Collection of Marguerite Steed Hoffman
Page 101

EDWARD KRASINSKI
Intervention, 1991
Mixed media and blue Scotch tape
39 ⅜ × 51 ⅛ × 5 ⅝ in. (100 × 129.9 × 14.3 cm)
The Rachofsky Collection
Pages 324–25

JIM LAMBIE
The Doors (Morrison Hotel), 2005
Wooden doors, mirrors, and gloss paint
80 ¼ × 75 ⅞ × 19 ½ in.
(203.8 × 192.7 × 49.5 cm)
The Rachofsky Collection and the Dallas
Museum of Art through the DMA/amfAR
Benefit Auction Fund
Page 355

LUISA LAMBRI
Untitled (Strathmore Apartments, #46), 2002
Laserchrome print
43 ¼ × 51 ⅛ in. (110 × 130 cm)
Edition: 1 of 5 + Artist's Proof
The Rachofsky Collection
Page 362

ANNETTE LAWRENCE
Moons, 1995–96
Mixed media on paper
Thirteen panels, unframed,
each: 15 × 10 in. (38.1 × 25.4 cm)
Overall, framed: 78 ¾ × 58 ¾ in.
(200 × 149.2 cm)
The Rachofsky Collection
Page 318; detail, page 299

PAULO ROBERTO LEAL
Des-Mov-Em, c. 1974
Acrylic box and rice paper
11 ¾ × 7 ⅞ × 7 ⅞ in. (29.8 × 20 × 20 cm)
The Rose Collection
Page 168

LEONILSON
Auto-retrato (Self-portrait), 1993
Steel, fabric, sewing, and embroidery
4 × 4 × 4 in. (10.2 × 10.2 × 10.2 cm)
The Rose Collection
Page 294

SHERRIE LEVINE
Monochromes After Mondrian: 1–16, 2012
Flashe on mahogany
Sixteen panels, each: 24 × 20 in. (61 × 50.8 cm)
Installation dimensions variable
Dallas Museum of Art through the
DMA/amfAR Benefit Auction Fund and
promised gift of The Rachofsky Collection
Pages 322–23

NATE LOWMAN
Broken Zip, 2010
Metal
Approximately 180 × 3 × 5 in.
(457.2 × 7.6 × 12.7 cm)
Installation dimensions variable
The Rachofsky Collection
Page 353

JORGE MACCHI
And, 2006
Newspaper cutting, pinned on paper
59⅜ × 79½ × 8¼ in.
(150.9 × 201.9 × 20.8 cm)
The Rose Collection
Page 313

PIERO MANZONI
Achrome, 1958
Kaolin on canvas
38¾ × 51⅛ in. (98.4 × 129.9 cm)
The Rachofsky Collection
Page 123

Achrome, 1960
Stitched velvet and board
31¼ × 23⅜ in. (79.4 × 59.4 cm)
The Rachofsky Collection
Page 100; detail, page 83

Achrome, 1962
Gravel and kaolin on canvas
28¾ × 24¾ in. (73 × 62.9 cm)
The Rose Collection
Page 37

AGNES MARTIN
Untitled, 1960
Oil on linen
12 × 12 in. (30.5 × 30.5 cm)
Collection of Robert and Marguerite Hoffman
Page 34

Untitled, 1960
Oil on linen
12 × 12 in. (30.5 × 30.5 cm)
The Rachofsky Collection
Page 35

Untitled #1, 1993
Acrylic and graphite on canvas
60 × 60 in. (152.4 × 152.4 cm)
The Rachofsky Collection
Page 51

GORDON MATTA-CLARK
Untitled (Food, Prince St. at Wooster St. NY), 1973
Wall fragment: wood, nails, metal, and pencil
19½ × 18⅜ × 4 in. (49.5 × 46.7 × 10.2 cm)
The Rose Collection
Page 254

Bronx Floors: Floor above, ceiling below, 1973
Gelatin silver prints
Two prints, framed: 26¾ × 20¾ in.
(67.9 × 52.7 cm)
The Rose Collection
Page 167

PAUL MCCARTHY
Face Painting—Floor, White Line, 1972 (printed 1989)
Gelatin silver prints
Two prints, each: 61 × 39 in. (154.9 × 99.1 cm)
Edition of 3 + 1 Artist's Proof
Sharon and Michael Young
Page 241

CILDO MEIRELES
Espelho Cego (Blind Mirror), 1970
Wood, rubber, and reversed metal in text relief
19¼ × 14⅛ × 7⅛ in. (48.9 × 35.9 × 18.1 cm)
1 of 3 versions
The Rose Collection
Page 161

ANNETTE MESSAGER
Mes voeux (My Vows), 1989
Acrylic on black-and-white photographs under glass and string
78¾ × 55 in. (200 × 139.7 cm)
The Rachofsky Collection
Page 289; detail, page vi

DONALD MOFFETT
Lot 031507 (Oolo), 2007
Oil, rayon, plated nickel, rabbit-skin glue, and polyvinyl acetate on linen in artist's painted wood frame
31½ × 27½ in. (80 × 69.8 cm)
The Rachofsky Collection
Page 335

REE MORTON
Wood Drawings, 1971
Felt-tip pen, pencil, acrylic, clay, sponge, and hardware on wood
Sixteen drawings—
height (range): 2½ to 17½ in. (6.3 to 44.4 cm);
length (range): 6 to 34 in. (15.2 to 86.4 cm)
The Rose Collection
Pages 164–65

SABURO MURAKAMI
Sakuhin (Work), c. 1970
Synthetic-resin paint, canvas, cotton, board, and mixed media
85⅜ × 48 × 3½ in. (217 × 122 × 9 cm)
The Rachofsky Collection
Page 213; detail, page 203

ELIZABETH MURRAY
Small Town, 1980
Oil on canvas
Six parts, overall: 132 × 130 in.
(335.3 × 330.2 cm)
The Rachofsky Collection
Page 217

NATSUYUKI NAKANISHI
Ningen no Chizu (Map of Human), 1959
Paint, enamel, and sand on plywood
48½ × 84¾ in. (123.2 × 215.3 cm)
The Rachofsky Collection
Page 151; detail, page 376

BRUCE NAUMAN
Untitled, 1965
Fiberglass and polyester resin
67¼ × 6¼ × 3⅛ in. (170.8 × 15.9 × 7.9 cm)
The Rose Collection
Page 259

Untitled (Lead Piece with Wedge), 1968
Lead, steel, and paint
4 × 47¼ × 47¼ in. (10.2 × 120 × 120 cm)
Dallas Museum of Art, anonymous gift
Page 157

BARNETT NEWMAN
Untitled Etching I (First Version), 1968
Etching
19 × 29½ in. (48.3 × 75 cm)
Edition: 8 of 27
Collection of Marguerite Steed Hoffman
Page 47

HÉLIO OITICICA
Untitled, 1970
Four shades of yellow ink on wood
33½ × 34⅝ × 41⅜ in. (85 × 88 × 105 cm)
The Rose Collection
Pages 162–63

CLAES OLDENBURG
Four Pies in a Glass Case, 1961
Muslin soaked in plaster over chicken wire, painted with enamel; glass case
5¼ × 30 × 9 in. (13.3 × 76.2 × 22.9 cm)
Collection of Robert and Marguerite Hoffman
Page 257

GABRIEL OROZCO
Inner Circles of the Wall, 1999
Plaster and graphite
Installation width: approximately 35 ft. (10.7 m)
The Rachofsky Collection, Collection of Deedie and Rusty Rose, and Dallas Museum of Art through the DMA/amfAR Benefit Auction Fund
Pages 336–37; detail, page 378

DAMIÁN ORTEGA
Tortillas Construction Module, 1998
Corn tortillas
Installation dimensions variable
The Rose Collection
Page 339

BLINKY PALERMO
Untitled, 1967–68
Casein paint on canvas
23⅝ × 70⅞ in. (60 × 180 cm)
The Rose Collection
Page 129; detail, page 118

LYGIA PAPE
Relief, 1954/56
Enamel and tempera on Eucatex and wood
15¾ × 15¾ × 2⅛ in. (40 × 40 × 5.5 cm)
The Rose Collection
Page 98

Livro Noite e Dia (Book Night and Day), 1963–76
Tempera on wood
Twelve pieces, each: 6¼ × 6¼ in.
(15.9 × 15.9 cm)
The Rose Collection
Page 103

GIUSEPPE PENONE
Albero di 5 metri (Tree of 5 Meters), 1969
Wood
196⅞ × 11¾ × 5⅞ in. (500 × 30 × 15 cm)
The Rose Collection
Page 255

Svolgere la propria pelle (To Unroll One's Skin), 1970
Copper and wood
Four panels; top left, bottom left, and top right, each: 31½ × 55⅛ in. (80 × 140 cm);
bottom right: 23⅝ × 55⅛ in. (60 × 140 cm)
The Rachofsky Collection
Page 242; detail, page 227

MANFRED PERNICE
Untitled (two cubes), 2008
MDF and paint
Two parts, each: 19¾ × 19¾ × 19¾ in.
(50.2 × 50.2 × 50.2 cm)
The Rose Collection
Page 338

GIANNI PIACENTINO
Metalloid Violet-Blue Vertical Wedge-Shaped Object (III), 1967–68
Polyester-coated and painted (water-based enamel, 2K acrylic matt clear) wood
114¼ × 4 × 15¾ in. (290 × 10 × 40 cm)
Collection of Marguerite Steed Hoffman
Page 69

CHARLOTTE POSENENSKE
Rasterbild (Halbkreise) (Grid [Semi-circles]), 1957
Study for a piece of wall art
Pencil on paper
15⅜ × 21⅞ in. (39 × 55.5 cm)
The Rose Collection
Page 122

Rasterbild (Halbkreise) (Grid [Semi-circles]), 1957
Flat model for a wall relief in the Dieburg District Court, horizontal rows of recessed circles with systematically varied, embossed semi-circle segments (not realized)
White paper and cardboard
15 × 24½ in. (38 × 62 cm)
The Rose Collection
Page 122

Faltung (Fold), 1966
Aluminum sprayed red, yellow, and blue
28⅛ × 26⅜ × 6¼ in. (71.5 × 67 × 16 cm)
The Rose Collection
Page 44; detail, page 4

Vierkantrohre (Square Tubes) Series D, 1967/2009, reconstruction
Sheet steel
Installation dimensions variable
The Rose Collection
Page 45

RICHARD PRINCE
Untitled (Check Painting), 2006
Acrylic and checks on canvas
108 × 156 in. (274.3 × 396.2 cm)
Collection of Marguerite Steed Hoffman
Pages 314–15

R. H. QUAYTMAN
Passing Through the Opposite of What It Approaches, Chapter 25 (after James Coleman's slide piece), 2012
Oil, tempera, silkscreen ink, and gesso on wood
Three parts—large: 37 × 60 in. (94.1 × 152.4 cm);
small: 12⅜ × 20 in. (31.4 × 50.8 cm);
shelf: 3 × 59½ × 1½ in. (7.6 × 151.1 × 3.8 cm)
The Rachofsky Collection
Page 357

MARKUS RAETZ
Opaques/Transparents, 2006
Galvanized wire with black patina, electric motor, aluminum pipe, and nylon thread
Two sculptures, each: ⅛ × 12⅜ × 21⅜ in.
(.4 × 31.4 × 54.3 cm)
Motor: 3 × 5¼ × 4 in.
(7.6 × 13.3 × 10.2 cm)
Edition: 6 of 6
The Rose Collection
Pages 220–21

CHARLES RAY
One-Stop Gallery, Iowa City, Iowa, 1971/1998
Concrete blocks and painted steel
Overall: 30 × 30 ft. (9.1 × 9.1 m)
Dallas Museum of Art, DMA/amfAR Benefit Auction Fund and the Contemporary Art Fund: Gift of Mr. and Mrs. Vernon E. Faulconer, Mr. and Mrs. Bryant M. Hanley Jr., Marguerite and Robert K. Hoffman, Cindy and Howard Rachofsky, Deedie and Rusty Rose, Gayle and Paul Stoffel, and two anonymous donors
Pages 264–65; details, pages 263 and 266

Rotating Circle, 1988
Electric motor with disc
Diameter: 9 in. (22.9 cm)
Dallas Museum of Art, fractional gift of The Rachofsky Collection
Page 288

AD REINHARDT
Untitled (black diptych), 1959–60
Oil on canvas
40 × 30 in. (101.6 × 76.2 cm)
The Rachofsky Collection
Page 99; detail, page 94

GERHARD RICHTER
Farbtafel (Colour Chart), 1966
Enamel on canvas
29½ × 19¾ in. (75 × 50 cm)
The Rose Collection
Page 107

MIMMO ROTELLA
Senza titolo (Untitled), 1954
Back of poster
23⅝ × 21⅝ in. (60 × 54.9 cm)
The Rachofsky Collection
Page 150; detail, page 379

ROBERT RYMAN
Untitled, 1961
Oil paint on stretched linen canvas
37⅞ × 37⅞ in. (96.2 × 96.2 cm)
The Rachofsky Collection
Page 36; detail, page 30

Lift, 2002
Oil on linen
43 × 43 in. (109.2 × 109.2 cm)
The Rose Collection
Page 171

Series #9 (White), 2004
Oil on canvas
53 × 53 in. (134.6 × 134.6 cm)
The Rachofsky Collection
Page 199

IRAN DO ESPÍRITO SANTO
Restless 23, 2004
Sandblasted glass and mirror
20 × 89 in. (50.8 × 226.1 cm)
The Rachofsky Collection
Pages 330–31

ALAN SARET
Green Wave of Air, 1968–69
Chicken wire
54 × 60 × 46 in. (137.2 × 152.4 × 116.8 cm)
Collection of Marguerite Steed Hoffman
Page 70; detail, page 374

MIRA SCHENDEL
Untitled, 1960s
Oil transfer drawing on thin Japanese paper
between painted transparent acrylic sheets
19⅝ × 19⅝ in. (49.8 × 49.8 cm)
Collection of Marguerite Steed Hoffman
Page 124

Untitled, 1963
Tempera on canvas
31⅛ × 39¾ in. (81 × 101 cm)
The Rose Collection
Page 104

Untitled, 1964
Plaster and tempera on wooden board
16½ × 13¾ × 1 in. (42 × 35 × 2.5 cm)
The Rose Collection
Page 105

Transformável (Transformable), 1970
Riveted strips of transparent acrylic
Approximately 25⅝ in. (65 cm)
The Rose Collection
Page 130; detail, page 111

NOBUO SEKINE
Phase No. 10, 1968
Wood, oil-based paint, and FRP
68½ × 72½ × 24¾ in. (174 × 184 × 63 cm)
The Rachofsky Collection and the Dallas
Museum of Art through the DMA/amfAR
Benefit Auction Fund
Page 158

Phase of Nothingness—Cloth and Stone,
1970/1994
Cloth, stone, rope, and panel
94½ × 89½ × 7⅞ in. (240 × 227.3 × 20 cm)
The Rachofsky Collection and the
Dallas Museum of Art through the
DMA/amfAR Benefit Auction Fund
Page 74; detail, page vii

RICHARD SERRA
Close Pin Prop, 1969–76
Rolled lead
Tube: 48 × 12 in. (121.9 × 30.5 cm)
Pole: 96 × 8 in. (243.8 × 20.3 cm)
The Rachofsky Collection
Page 71; detail, page 55

JOEL SHAPIRO
Untitled (Fingerprints), 1969–70
Ink on paper
17½ × 17½ in. (44.4 × 44.4 cm)
The Rose Collection
Page 251

Untitled (Bronze House), 1973–74
Bronze
6 × 5 × 4⅛ in. (15.2 × 12.7 × 10.5 cm)
Edition: 2 of 3
Collection of Robert and Marguerite Hoffman
Pages 214–15

SHOZO SHIMAMOTO
Work-(Hole 05)-, 1950
White paint on newspaper
19¼ × 13¾ in. (49 × 35 cm)
The Rose Collection
Page 149; detail, page 135

PAUL SIETSEMA
Painter's Mussel 6, 2011
Ink on paper in artist's frame
72¼ × 71¼ in. (183.5 × 181 cm)
The Rachofsky Collection
Page 332

LEON POLK SMITH
Black angles on white, 1947
Oil on canvas mounted on plywood
Panel: 36 × 12 in. (91.4 × 30.5 cm)
Canvas: 33¼ × 8¾ in. (84.5 × 22.2 cm)
The Rose Collection
Page 121

TONY SMITH
Untitled, c. 1934–36
Oil on canvas board
9 × 7 in. (22.9 × 17.8 cm)
The Rose Collection
Page 97

ROBERT SMITHSON
Ziggurat, 1966
Painted and polished metal
27½ × 27½ × 24 in. (69.9 × 69.9 × 61 cm)
The Rose Collection
Page 67; detail, page 8

Mirrors and Shelly Sand, 1969–70
Mirrors and beach sand with shells or pebbles
Fifty mirrors, back to back, each: 12 × 48 in.
(30.5 × 121.9 cm)
Installation length: approximately 28 ft. (8.5 m)
Dallas Museum of Art, gift of an anonymous
donor; the Vin and Caren Prothro Foundation;
Rusty and Deedie Rose in memory of
Vin Prothro and in honor of his cherished
grandchildren, Lillian Lee Clark and Annabel
Caren Clark; The Eugene McDermott
Foundation; Dr. and Mrs. Mark L. Lemmon;
American Consolidated Media; Bear/Hunter;
and donors to the C. Vincent Prothro
Memorial Foundation
Pages 72–73

FRANCES STARK
*The world becomes a private world
and shines like a rainbow*, 1998
Carbon, oil, and permanent marker on paper
87 × 60 in. (221 × 152.4 cm)
The Rachofsky Collection
Page 361

FRANK STELLA
Valparaiso Green, 1963
Metallic paint on canvas
78 × 180 in. (198.1 × 457.2 cm)
Collection of Robert and Marguerite Hoffman
Pages 38–39

JIRO TAKAMATSU
Cube 6 + 3, 1968
Lacquer on wood
13 × 13 × 13 in. (33 × 33 × 33 cm)
The Rachofsky Collection and the Dallas
Museum of Art through the DMA/amfAR
Benefit Auction Fund
Page 159

Oneness of Paper, 1970
Colored paper on Kent paper
24⅜ × 16 in. (62 × 40.5 cm)
The Rachofsky Collection and the Dallas
Museum of Art, gift of Mrs. Jiro Takamatsu
Page 160

Oneness of Concrete, 1971
Concrete
10⅝ × 19¾ × 19¾ in. (27 × 50.2 × 50.2 cm)
Amy and Vernon Faulconer and
The Rachofsky Collection
Page 166; detail, page viii

Shadow of Nail No. 400, 1975
Lacquer and iron nail on wood panel
12⅞ × 9¼ in. (32.7 × 23.5 cm)
The Rachofsky Collection
Page 131

CHEYNEY THOMPSON
Pedestal (P), 2012
MDF and HPL
2 in. × 33 ft. 3 in. × 2 in.
(5.1 cm × 10.1 m × 5.1 cm)
The Rachofsky Collection
Page 365, detail; page 350

ANNE TRUITT
Valley Forge, 1963
Acrylic on wood
60½ × 60¼ × 12 in. (153.7 × 153 × 30.5 cm)
The Rachofsky Collection
Page 40; detail, page 23

RICHARD TUTTLE
Sail, 1964
Acrylic on wood
10 × 40 × 3 in. (25.4 × 101.6 × 7.6 cm)
The Rose Collection
Page 65

Equals, 1964–65
Acrylic on plywood
39 × 47¼ × 1½ in. (99.1 × 120 × 3.8 cm)
Collection of Robert and Marguerite Hoffman
Page 66

1st Wire Bridge, 1971
Wire and nails
37½ × 38½ in. (95.2 × 97.8 cm)
The Rachofsky Collection
Page 75; detail, page 62

LUC TUYMANS
Slide #1, 2002
Oil on canvas
80⅛ × 52¾ in. (203.5 × 134 cm)
Amy and Vernon Faulconer and
The Rachofsky Collection
Page 334

GÜNTHER UECKER
Weisses Phantom, 1962
Painted nails and oil on canvas on panel
43⅜ × 78¾ in. (110.2 × 200 cm)
The Rachofsky Collection
Pages 186–87; detail, page 175

LEE UFAN
From Point, 1978
Glue and stone pigment on canvas
71½ × 89⅜ in. (181.6 × 227 cm)
The Rachofsky Collection and the Dallas
Museum of Art through the DMA/amfAR
Benefit Auction Fund
Page 197; detail, page 377

DAVID WATKINS
Necklace, 1977
Gold
7¼ × 8¼ × ¾ in. (18.4 × 21 × 1.9 cm)
Dallas Museum of Art, gift of Edward W. and
Deedie Potter Rose, formerly Inge Asenbaum
Collection, Gallery Am Graben in Vienna
Page 281

RACHEL WHITEREAD
Untitled (Air Bed), 1992
Plastic and polystyrene
8⅝ × 47¼ × 76⅜ in. (21.9 × 120 × 194 cm)
Collection of Robert and Marguerite Hoffman
Page 293

HANNAH WILKE
Untitled, 1975–78
Sixty ceramic sculptures and wooden board
Overall: 32 × 32 in. (81.3 × 81.3 cm)
Vitrine: 38 × 35 × 35 in. (96.5 × 88.9 × 88.9 cm)
Collection of Marguerite Steed Hoffman
Page 243; detail, page 10

JACKIE WINSOR
Burnt Paper Piece, 1981–82
Wood, reams of paper, and hydrostone
32⅛ × 32⅛ × 32⅛ in. (81.6 × 81.6 × 81.6 cm)
Collection of Robert and Marguerite Hoffman
Page 218; detail, page 210

CHRISTOPHER WOOL
Untitled, 1990
Enamel and acrylic on aluminum
96 × 64 in. (243.8 × 162.6 cm)
Collection of Marguerite Steed Hoffman
Page 291

JIRO YOSHIHARA
Work, 1965
Oil on canvas
71 × 90 in. (180.3 × 228.6 cm)
The Rachofsky Collection
Page 156

JOE ZUCKER
Untitled Mosaic (Three Figures), 1972
Acrylic, cotton, and Rhoplex on canvas
60 × 60 in. (152.4 × 152.4 cm)
The Rachofsky Collection
Page 244

Albers, Josef. *Interaction of Color*. Rev. and exp. New Haven and London: Yale University Press, 2013.

Ammer, Manuela, et al. *Ree Morton: Be a Place, Place an Image, Imagine a Poem*. Madrid: Museo Nacional Centro de Arte Reina Sofía, 2015.

Armstrong, Elizabeth, Johanna Burton, and Dave Hickey. *Mary Heilmann: To Be Someone*. Exh. cat. Orange County Museum of Art, Newport Beach, CA. Munich and London: Prestel Verlag, 2007.

Asakura, Yuichiro, et al. *Jiro Takamatsu: All Drawings*. Hiroshima: Daiwa Press, 2009.

Barson, Tanya, and Taisa Palhares, eds. *Mira Schendel*. Exh. cat. Tate Modern, London. London: Tate Publishing in association with Pinacoteca do Estado de São Paulo, 2013.

Bedford, Christopher. *Mark Bradford*. Exh. cat. Columbus, OH: Wexner Center for the Arts, 2010.

———. *Paul Sietsema*. Exh. cat. Columbus, OH: Wexner Center for the Visual Arts, 2013.

Bell, Tiffany. *Dan Flavin: Series and Progressions*. Exh. cat. David Zwirner Gallery, New York. Göttingen, Germany: Steidl, 2010.

Bellini, Andrea. *Gianni Piacentino*. Exh. cat. Centre d'art contemporaine, Geneva. Geneva: JRP/Ringier, 2013.

Berswordt-Wallrabe, Silke von. *Lee Ufan: Encounters with the Other*. Translated by Michael E. Foster. Göttingen, Germany: Steidl, 2007.

Blazwick, Iwona, et al. *Adventures of the Black Square: Abstract Art and Society, 1915–2015*. Exh. cat. Whitechapel Gallery, London. Munich: Prestel Verlag, 2015.

Blistène, Bernard, and Flaminio Gualdoni. *Dadamaino*. Exh. cat. Galerie Tornabuoni Art, Paris. Poggibonsi, Siena, Italy: Forma, 2013.

Boehm, Gottfried, Ellsworth Kelly, and Viola Weigel. *Ellsworth Kelly: In-Between Spaces; Works, 1956–2002*. Exh. cat. Fondation Beyler, Riehen, Germany. Ostfildern-Ruit, Germany: Hatje Cantz, 2002.

Bonami, Francesco, Michel Gauthier, and Ilina Koralova. *Jeppe Hein: Until Now*. London: Koenig Books, 2006.

Bonito, Achille, et al. *Shozo Shimamoto: Opere, 1950–2011, Oriente e Occidente; Works, 1950–2011, East and West*. Turin: Umberto Allemandi, 2011.

Borja-Villel, Manuel J., and Teresa Velázquez. *Lygia Pape: Magnetized Space*. Exh. cat. Madrid: Museo Nacional Centro de Arte Reina Sofía, 2011.

Brett, Guy, ed. *Cildo Meireles*. London: Tate Publishing, 2008.

———, and Suzanne Cotter. *Force Fields: Phases of the Kinetic*. Exh. cat. Barcelona: Museu d'Art Contemporani, 2000.

Brinson, Katherine. *Christopher Wool*. Exh. cat. New York: Guggenheim Museum, 2013.

Broodthaers, Marie-Puck, ed. *Marcel Broodthaers*. New York: Distributed Art Publishers, 2013.

Bürgi, Bernhard Mendes, and James Rondeau, eds. *Charles Ray: Sculpture, 1997–2014*. Exh. cat. Kunstmuseum, Basel, and Art Institute of Chicago. Ostfildern-Ruit, Germany: Hatje Cantz, 2014.

Burton, Johanna, and Elisabeth Sussman. *Sherrie Levine: Mayhem*. Exh. cat. New York: Whitney Museum of American Art, 2012.

Busine, Laurent, and Didier Semyn, eds. *Giuseppe Penone: Forty Years of Creation*. New Haven: Yale University Press, 2012.

Butler, Cornelia H., and Luis Pérez-Oramas, eds. *Lygia Clark: The Abandonment of Art, 1948–1988*. Exh. cat. New York: Museum of Modern Art, 2014.

Cadot, Farideh, and Marie-Cécile Miessner, eds. *Markus Raetz: Prints, Sculptures*. Exh. cat. Paris: Bibliothèque Nationale de France, 2011.

Cameron, Dan, Amelia Jones, and Anthony Vidler. *Paul McCarthy*. Exh. cat. Museum of Contemporary Art, Los Angeles, and New Museum of Contemporary Art, New York. Ostfildern-Ruit, Germany: Hatje Cantz, 2000.

Celant, Germano. *Michael Heizer*. Exh. cat. Translated by Stephen Sartarelli. Milan: Fondazione Prada, 1997.

———. *Piero Manzoni: Catalogo Generale*. Milan: Skira, 2004.

Chaimovich, Felipe. *Iran do Espírito Santo*. São Paulo: Cosac and Naify, 2000.

Charlet, Nicolas. *Yves Klein*. Translated by Michael Taylor. Paris: Adam Biro, 2000.

Conkelton, Sheryl, and Carol S. Eliel. *Annette Messager*. Exh. cat. Los Angeles County Museum of Art and other venues. New York: Museum of Modern Art, 1995.

Cooke, Lynne. *Agnes Martin*. Exh. cat. New York: Dia Art Foundation, 2011.

———, Karen Kelly, and Barbara Schröder. *Blinky Palermo: Retrospective, 1964–1977*. Exh. cat. New York: Dia Art Foundation, 2010.

———, et al. *Alighiero Boetti: Game Plan*. Exh. cat. New York: Museum of Modern Art, 2012.

Cooper, Harry, and Megan R. Luke. *Frank Stella, 1958*. Exh. cat. Harvard University Art Museums, Cambridge, MA. London: Yale University Press, 2006.

Danto, Arthur C., and Ralph Rugoff. *Tom Friedman*. Exh. cat. Gagosian Gallery, London. New Haven: Yale University Press, 2008.

Davies, Hugh M., and Robert Irwin. *Robert Irwin: Primaries and Secondaries*. Exh. cat. San Diego: Museum of Contemporary Art San Diego, 2008.

Deitch, Jeffrey. *The Painting Factory: Abstraction after Warhol*. Exh. cat. Museum of Contemporary Art, Los Angeles. New York: Skira Rizzoli, 2012.

Diserens, Corinne. *Gordon Matta-Clark*. New York: Phaidon, 2003.

Dziewior, Yilmaz, et al. *Gabriel Orozco: Natural Motion*. Exh. cat. Bregenz, Austria, and Stockholm: Kunsthaus Bregenz and Moderna Museet, 2014.

Fer, Briony. *The Infinite Line: Re-making Art After Modernism*. New Haven: Yale University Press, 2004.

Fernandes, Joao, Paulo Venancio Filho, and Fernando Gerheim. *Fernanda Gomes*. Exh. cat. Porto, Portugal: Museu Serralves, 2006.

Fiz, Alberto. *Mimmo Rotella: Roma, Parigi, New York*. Milan: Skira, 2009.

Fleischner, Richard. *Richard Fleischner: Works 1963–2011, Material / Process / Place*. Exh. cat. Knoedler Gallery, New York. New York: Knoedler, 2011.

Flood, Richard, et al. *Unmonumental: The Object in the 21st Century*. Exh. cat. New Museum, New York. New York: Phaidon, 2007.

Frankel, David. *Richard Serra: Early Work*. Exh. cat. New York: David Zwirner, 2013.

Fuchs, Rudi. *Gilbert & George: The Complete Pictures, 1971–2005*. Exh. cat. London: Tate, 2007.

Gavlak, Sarah. *Joe Zucker: Ravenna*. Exh. cat. New York: GBE (Modern) and Gavlak Projects, 2003.

Glimcher, Arne. *Agnes Martin: Paintings, Writings, Remembrances*. New York: Phaidon, 2012.

Godfrey, Mark, and Nicholas Serota. *Gerhard Richter: Panorama*. Exh. cat. London: Tate Publishing, 2011.

———, and R. H. Quaytman. *R. H. Quaytman: Dalet Chapter 24*. Exh. cat. Mönchengladbach, Germany: Museum Abteiberg Mönchengladbach, 2012.

Goldberger, Paul. *Frank Stella: Painting into Architecture*. Exh. cat. New York: Metropolitan Museum of Art, 2007.

Gottschaller, Pia. *Lucio Fontana; The Artist's Materials*. Los Angeles: Getty Conservation Institute, 2012.

Gray, Zoë. *Alexandre da Cunha*. Exh. cat. CRG Gallery, New York, and other venues. Rio de Janeiro: Editora de Livros Cobogó, 2012.

Graze, Sue, and Kathy Halbreich. *Elizabeth Murray: Paintings and Drawings*. Exh. cat. Dallas Museum of Art. New York: Harry N. Abrams, 1987.

Greenberg, Kerryn. *Meschac Gaba: Museum of Contemporary African Art*. Exh. cat. Tate Modern, London. London: Tate Publishing, 2013.

Grove, Jeffrey, and Olga Viso. *Jim Hodges: Give More Than You Take*. Exh. cat. Dallas Museum of Art and other venues. Dallas, TX: Dallas Museum of Art, 2013.

Grynsztejn, Madeleine, and Helen Molesworth. *Luc Tuymans*. Exh. cat. Wexner Center for the Arts, Columbus, OH, and other venues. San Francisco: San Francisco Museum of Modern Art, 2009.

Heinrich, Christoph. *Mona Hatoum*. Exh. cat. Hamburger Kunsthalle, Hamburg. Ostfildern-Ruit, Germany: Hatje Cantz, 2004.

Hileman, Kristen, and Anne Truitt. *Perception and Reflection*. Exh. cat. Washington, DC: Hirshhorn Museum and Sculpture Garden, Smithsonian Institution, 2009.

Hirai, Shoichi, et al. *Norio Imai*. Exh. cat. Axel Vervoordt Gallery, Antwerp. Gent, Belgium: AsaMER, Paper Kunsthalle, 2013.

Hollein, Max, and Klaus Ottmann. *James Lee Byars: Life, Love, and Death*. Ostfildern-Ruit, Germany: Hatje Cantz, 2004.

Iversen, Margaret, Douglas Crimp, and Homi K. Bhabha. *Mary Kelly*. London: Phaidon, 1997.

Jacobson, Heidi Zuckerman. *Sergej Jensen*. Exh. cat. MoMA PS1, New York. Berlin: Distanz Verlag, 2011.

———, and Barry Schwabsky. *Mark Grotjahn*. Exh. cat. Aspen, CO: Aspen Art Museum, 2012.

Johnson, Matt, and Pascal Spengemann. *Matt Johnson: Small Sculptures*. Artists Book Series. Los Angeles: Wood Kusaka Studios, 2012.

Kaiser, Philipp, and Burkhard Brunn. *Charlotte Posenenske: Die Frühen Arbeiten / The Early Works*. Berlin: Distanz, 2012.

Kamiyama, Ryoko, and Hitoshi Yamamura. *Takamatsu Jiro: Universe of His Thought*. Exh. cat. Tokyo: Fuchu Art Museum; Fukuoka, Japan: Kitakyushu Municipal Museum of Art, 2004.

Kertess, Klaus. *Alan Saret: Matter into Aether*. Exh. cat. Newport Beach: Newport Harbor Art Museum, 1982.

Kiessler, Lena. *Edward Krasinski*. Exh. cat. New York: Anton Kern Gallery, 2002.

Krystof, Doris, and Jessica Morgan. *Martin Kippenberger*. Exh. cat. Tate Modern, London, and Kunstsammlung Nordrhein-Westfalen, Germany. London: Tate Publishing, 2006.

Kuri, Gabriel. *Damián Ortega: Reading Landscapes*. Exh. cat. Seoul: Kukje Gallery, 2014.

Lambie, Jim, et al. *Voidoid*. Glasgow and New York: Modern Institute and Anton Kern Gallery 2004.

Lewallen, Constance M., et. al. *A Rose Has No Teeth: Bruce Nauman in the 1960s*. Exh. cat. Berkeley Art Museum, Berkeley, CA. Los Angeles: University of California Press, 2007.

Liden, Hanna, et al. *Nate Lowman: The Natriot Act*. Exh. cat. Oslo: Astrup Fearnley Museum of Modern Art, 2009.

Lind, Maria, ed. *Abstraction*. Documents of Contemporary Art. London: Whitechapel Gallery, 2013.

Lippard, Lucy. *Judy Chicago*. Exh. cat. National Museum of Women in the Arts, Washington, DC. New York: Watson-Guptill and the Elizabeth A. Sackler Foundation, 2002.

Maraniello, Gianfranco, and Andrea Villani, eds. *Giovanni Anselmo*. Exh. cat. Galleria d'arte moderna, Bologna, Italy. Turin: Hopefulmonster, 2007.

Mesquita, Ivo. *Leonilson: use, é lindo, eu garanto*. São Paulo: Cosac and Naify, 1997.

Meyer, James, ed. *Minimalism*. Themes and Movements (series). London: Phaidon, 2000.

Meyer-Hermann, Eva. *Paul McCarthy: Brain Dream Box*. Exh. cat. Van Abbemuseum, Eindhoven, The Netherlands. Düsseldorf: Richter Verlag, 2004.

Mignot, Dorine, Eleanor Louis, and Toni Stooss, eds. *Gary Hill . . .* Exh. cat. Stedelijk Museum, Amsterdam, and other venues. Amsterdam and Vienna: Stedelijk Museum and Kunsthalle Wien, 1992.

Monk, Bob. *Richard Artschwager*. Exh. cat. New York: Gagosian Gallery, 2008.

Morris, Frances, ed. *Louise Bourgeois*. Exh. cat. Tate Modern, London. London: Tate Publishing, 2007.

Müller, Christopher, and Jay Sanders. *Tony Conrad: Yellow Movies*. Exh. cat. New York: Greene Naftali, 2008.

Mullins, Charlotte. *Rachel Whiteread*. London: Tate Publishing, 2004.

Munder, Heike, and Philip Ursprung. *Heidi Bucher*. Exh. cat. Migros Museum für Gegenwartskunst, Zurich. Zurich: JRP/Ringier, 2005.

Munroe, Alexandra. *Lee Ufan: Marking Infinity*. Exh. cat. New York: Guggenheim Museum, 2011.

Nye, Tim. *Peter Alexander: Resin Works, 1965–2009*. Exh. cat. New York: Foundation 20 21/Nyehaus, 2009.

O'Hare, Mary Kate. *Constructivist Spirit: Abstract Art in South and North America, 1920s–50s*. Exh. cat. Newark Museum, Newark, NJ. San Francisco: Pomegranate, 2010.

Oliver, Valerie Cassel, et al. *Donald Moffett: The Extravagant Vein*. Exh. cat. Contemporary Arts Museum, Houston, and other venues. New York: Skira Rizzoli, 2011.

Olsen, Valerie Loupe. *Annette Lawrence: Theory*. Exh. cat. Houston, TX: Museum of Fine Arts, Glassell School of Art, 2002.

Olveira, Manuel, and Gabriel Pérez-Barreiro. *Jorge Macchi: Anatomía de Melancolía*. Exh. cat. Centro Galego de Arte Contemporánea, Santiago de Compostela, Spain. Corunna, Spain: Xunta de Galicia, 2009.

Osaka City Museum of Modern Art, et al., eds. *Jiro Yoshihara: A Centenary Retrospective*. Exh. cat. ATC Museum, Osaka, and other venues. Tokyo: Asahi Shimbun, 2005.

Pacheco, Marcelo E. *Victor Grippo: Una Retrospectiva; Obras, 1971–2001*. Exh. cat. Buenos Aires: Malba—Colección Costantini, 2004.

Paik, Tricia. *Ellsworth Kelly*. London: Phaidon Press, 2015.

Pedrosa, Ariano, et al. *Luisa Lambri: Interiors*. Exh. cat. Ivorypress Art + Book Space 1, Madrid. London: Ivorypress, 2011.

Pérez-Barreiro, Gabriel. *The Geometry of Hope: Latin American Art from the Patricia Phelps de Cisneros Collection*. Exh. cat. Blanton Museum of Art, Austin. Austin: University of Texas at Austin, 2007.

Princenthal, Nancy. *Hannah Wilke*. Munich: Prestel Verlag, 2010.

Ramírez, Mari Carmen. *Hélio Oiticica: The Body of Color*. Exh. cat. Museum of Fine Arts, Houston, and Tate Modern, London. London: Tate Publishing, 2007.

Ratcliff, Carter, *Leon Polk Smith: American Painter*. Exh. cat. Brooklyn, NY: Brooklyn Museum, 1996.

Ribas, João, et al. *Cheyney Thompson: Metric, Pedestal, Cabengo, Landlord, Récit*. Exh. cat. MIT Visual Arts Center, Cambridge, MA. London: Koenig Books, 2012.

Robinson, Julia E. *Claes Oldenburg: Early Work*. Exh. cat. New York: Zwirner and Wirth, 2005.

Rothkopf, Scott. *Wade Guyton OS*. Exh. cat. New York: Whitney Museum of American Art, 2012.

Saldanha, Claudia, and Luiz Guilherme Vergara. *Paulo Roberto Leal: Da Matéria Nasce a Forma*. Exh. cat. Niterói, Brazil: Museu de Arte Contemporânea de Niterói, 2007.

Schiff, Richard, Carol C. Mancusi-Ungaro, and Heidi Colsman-Freyberger. *Barnet Newman: A Catalogue Raisonné*. New York and New Haven: Barnett Newman Foundation and Yale University Press, 2004.

Schwarz, Dieter, ed. *John Chamberlain: Papier Paradisio; Drawings, Collages, Reliefs, Paintings*. Exh. cat. Kunstmuseum Winterthur, Germany. Düsseldorf: Richter Verlag, 2005.

Serafini, Giuliano. *Burri: The Measure and the Phenomenon*. Milan: Charta, 1999.

Serban, Alina, et al. *Geta Brătescu: Atelierul / The Studio*. Berlin: Sternberg Press, 2013.

Serota, Nicholas. *Donald Judd*. Exh. cat. Tate Modern, London and other venues. New York: Distributed Art Publishers, 2004.

Simms, Matthew. *Robert Irwin: Notes Toward a Conditional Art*. Los Angeles: J. Paul Getty Trust, 2011.

Sobel, Dean, Peter Schjeldahl, and John Yau. *Jackie Winsor*. Exh. cat. Milwaukee: Milwaukee Art Museum, 1991.

Spector, Nancy. *Félix González-Torres*. Exh. cat. New York: Guggenheim Museum, 2007.

Sretenovic, Vesela. *Robert Ryman: Variations + Improvisations*. Exh. cat. Washington, DC: Phillips Collection, 2010.

[Stark, Frances]. *Collected Writings, 1993–2003 / Frances Stark*. London: Book Works, 2003.

Storr, Robert, et al. *Tony Smith: Architect, Painter, Sculptor*. Exh. cat. New York: Museum of Modern Art, 1998.

Stringari, Carol. *Imageless: The Scientific Study and Experimental Treatment of an Ad Reinhardt Black Painting*. New York: Guggenheim Museum, 2008.

Südbeck, Annette. *Manfred Pernice: Sculpturama*. Vienna and Berlin: Wiener Secession and Revolver, 2011.

Teicher, Hendel, and Michael Brenson. *Joel Shapiro: Sculpture and Drawing*. New York: Harry N. Abrams, 1998.

Tiampo, Ming, and Alexandra Munroe. *Gutai: Splendid Playground*. Exh. cat. New York: Guggenheim Museum, 2013.

Tolnay, Alexander, ed. *Günther Uecker: Twenty Chapters*. Ostfildern-Ruit, Germany: Hatje Cantz, 2006.

Tomii, Reiko, and Ikegami Tsukasa. *Murakami Saburo: Through the '70s*. Exh. cat. Osaka: Artcourt Gallery, 2013.

Tsai, Eugenie, and Cornelia H. Butler. *Robert Smithson*. Exh. cat. Museum of Contemporary Art, Los Angeles. Berkeley, CA: University of California Press, 2004.

Tuttle, Richard, et al. *Richard Tuttle: I Don't Know. The Weave of Textile Language*. Exh. cat. Tate Modern, London. London: Tate Publishing, 2015.

Umemura, Yumi. *Natsuyuki Nakanishi: Chiasme*. Exh. cat. Tokyo: SCAI the Bathhouse, 2014.

Vischer, Theodora, ed. *Robert Gober: Sculptures and Installations, 1979–2007*. Exh. cat. Schaulager Basel. Göttingen, Germany: Steidl, 2007.

Wagner, Bruce, and John McWhinnie. *Richard Prince: Check Paintings*. Exh. cat. Beverly Hills, CA: Gagosian Gallery, 2005.

Wirz, Renata, and Federico Sardella. *Enrico Castellani: Catalogo Ragionato, 1955–2005*. Milan: Archivio Castellanti, 2012.

Wylie, Charles. *Robert Ryman*. Exh. cat. Dallas, TX: Dallas Museum of Art, 2006.

GEOMETRIES ON AND OFF THE GRID:
ART FROM 1950 TO THE PRESENT
Published by The Warehouse

The Warehouse
14105 Inwood Road
Dallas, TX 75244
www.thewarehousedallas.org

Editor: Allan Schwartzman
Copyeditor: Frances Bowles
Publication Manager: Meg Smith Gratch

Creative Direction and Design: McCall Associates, NY
Typeset in Quotient, designed by Terminal Design, Brooklyn
Printed on Galerie Art Volume and Neptune Bianco Artico
Color separation, printing, and binding by Brizzolis S.A.,
Madrid

ISBN. 978-0-692-53618-6

Jacket: Frank Stella, *Valparaiso Green*, 1963. Metallic paint on
canvas. 78 × 180 in. (198.1 × 457.2 cm)

Details:
Page i: Joseph Albers, *Homage to the Square (732)*, 1961.
Oil on Masonite. Panel: 30⅛ × 30⅛ in. (76.5 × 76.5 cm).
Framed: 30⅝ × 30⅝ × 1¼ in. (77.8 × 77.8 × 3.2 cm)

Page ii: Norio Imai, *White Ceremony/Toward #1*, 1966–70.
Acrylic, cotton cloth, and plastic pattern. 28½ × 15½ × 3⅛ in.
(72.5 × 39.5 × 8 cm)

Page iii: Lucio Fontana, *Concetto spaziale, la fine di Dio (Spatial
Concept, The End of God)*, 1964. Oil on canvas. 70 × 48½ in.
(177.8 × 123.2 cm)

Page iv: Sergio Camargo, *Relief No. 262*, 1969. Wood relief
and paint. Panel: 47¼ × 39⅜ × 3⅛ in. (120 × 100 × 7.9 cm)

Page v: John Chamberlain, *Rap Psalm II*, 1999. Painted chromium
and painted steel. 103½ × 59 × 47 in. (262.9 × 149.9 × 119.4 cm)

Page vi: Annette Messager, *Mes voeux (My Vows)*, 1989.
Acrylic on black-and-white photographs under glass and string.
78¾ × 55 in. (200 × 139.7 cm)

Page vii: Nobuo Sekine, *Phase of Nothingness—Cloth and
Stone*, 1970/1994. Cloth, stone, rope, and panel.
94½ × 89½ × 7⅞ in. (240 × 227.3 × 20 cm)

Page viii: Jiro Takamatsu, *Oneness of Concrete*, 1971.
Concrete. 10⅝ × 19¾ × 19¾ in. (27 × 50.2 × 50.2 cm)

Page 4: Charlotte Posenenske, *Faltung (Fold)*, 1966.
Aluminum sprayed red, yellow, and blue. 28⅛ × 26⅜ × 6¼ in.
(71.5 × 67 × 16 cm)

Page 8: Robert Smithson, *Ziggurat*, 1966. Painted and polished
metal. 27½ × 27½ × 24 in. (69.9 × 69.9 × 61 cm)

Page 10: Hannah Wilke, *Untitled*, 1975–78. Sixty ceramic sculptures
and wooden board. Overall: 32 × 32 in. (81.3 × 81.3 cm).
Vitrine: 38 × 35 × 35 in. (96.5 × 88.9 × 88.9 cm)

Page 23: Anne Truitt, *Valley Forge*, 1963. Acrylic on wood.
60½ × 60¼ × 12 in. (153.7 × 153 × 30.5 cm)

Page 30: Robert Ryman, *Untitled*, 1961. Oil paint on stretched
linen canvas. 37⅞ × 37⅞ in. (96.2 × 96.2 cm)

Page 55: Richard Serra, *Close Pin Prop*, 1969–76. Rolled lead.
Tube: 48 × 12 in. (121.9 × 30.5 cm). Pole: 96 × 8 in.
(243.8 × 20.3 cm)

Page 62: Richard Tuttle, *1st Wire Bridge*, 1971. Wire and nails.
37½ × 38½ in. (95.2 × 97.8 cm)

Page 83: Piero Manzoni, *Achrome*, 1960. Stitched velvet and
board. 31¼ × 23⅜ in. (79.4 × 59.4 cm)

Page 94: Ad Reinhardt, *Untitled (black diptych)*, 1959–60.
Oil on canvas. 40 × 30 in. (101.6 × 76.2 cm)

Page 111: Mira Schendel, *Transformável (Transformable)*, 1970.
Riveted strips of transparent acrylic. Approximately 25⅝ in.
(65 cm)

Page 118: Blinky Palermo, *Untitled*, 1967–68. Casein paint on
canvas. 23⅝ × 70⅞ in. (60 × 180 cm)

Page 135: Shozo Shimamoto, *Work-(Hole 05)-*, 1950. White
paint on newspaper. 19¼ × 13¾ in. (49 × 35 cm)

Page 146: Victor Grippo, *Vida, Muerte, Resurrección (Life,
Death, Resurrection)*, 1980. Five hollow geometrical lead bodies;
five hollow geometrical lead bodies filled with black and red
beans; water; glass box. Overall: 19½ × 47½ × 31½ in.
(49.5 × 120.6 × 80 cm)

Page 175: Günther Uecker, *Weisses Phantom*, 1962.
Painted nails and oil on canvas on panel. 43⅜ × 78¾ in.
(110.2 × 200 cm)

Page 182: Dadamaino, *Volume a modulazioni sfasate (Volume
of Displaced Modules)*, 1960. Sheets of plastic applied on
superimposed frames. 15¾ × 11¾ in. (40 × 30 cm)

Page 203: Saburo Murakami, *Sakuhin (Work)*, c. 1970.
Synthetic-resin paint, canvas, cotton, board, and mixed media.
85⅛ × 48 × 3½ in. (217 × 122 × 9 cm)

Page 210: Jackie Winsor, *Burnt Paper Piece*, 1981–82. Wood,
reams of paper, and hydrostone. 32⅛ × 32⅛ × 32⅛ in.
(81.6 × 81.6 × 81.6 cm)

Page 227: Giuseppe Penone, *Svolgere la propria pelle (To Unroll
One's Skin)*, 1970. Copper and wood. Four panels; top left,
bottom left, and top right, each: 31½ × 55⅛ in. (80 × 140 cm);
bottom right: 23⅝ × 55⅛ in. (60 × 140 cm)

Page 238: Judy Chicago, *The Liberation of the Great Ladies*,
1973. Sprayed acrylic and ink on canvas. 40 × 40 in.
(101.6 × 101.6 cm)

Pages 263 and 266: Charles Ray, *One-Stop Gallery, Iowa City,
Iowa*, 1971/1998. Concrete blocks and painted steel.
Overall: 30 × 30 ft. (9.1 × 9.1 m)

Page 271: Robert Gober, *Untitled*, 2003–2005. Bronze and oil
paint. 9 × 46½ × 61 in. (22.9 × 118.1 × 154.9 cm)

Page 278: Félix González-Torres, *"Untitled" (7 Days of Bloodworks)*, 1988. Gesso, acrylic, and graphite on canvas. Seven
parts, each: 20 × 16 in. (50.8 × 40.6 cm). Overall dimensions
vary with installation

Page 299: Annette Lawrence, *Moons*, 1995–96. Mixed
media on paper. Thirteen panels, unframed, each: 15 × 10 in.
(38.1 × 25.4 cm). Overall, framed: 78¾ × 58¾ in.
(200 × 149.2 cm)

Page 310: Mark Bradford, *A Truly Rich Man is One Whose
Children Run Into His Arms When His Hands are Empty*,
2008. Mixed media collage on canvas. 102 × 144 in.
(259.1 × 365.8 cm)

Page 343: Alexandre Da Cunha, *Arcadia*, 2007. Cleaning mop
head, bathroom mat, wool, tapestry canvas, and wooden
stretcher. 72½ × 53½ in. (184 × 136 cm)

Page 350: Cheyney Thompson, *Pedestal (P)*, 2012. MDF and
HPL. 2 in. × 33 ft. 3 in. × 2 in. (5.1 cm × 10.1 m × 5.1 cm)

Page 374: Alan Saret, *Green Wave of Air*, 1968–69. Chicken
wire. 54 × 60 × 46 in. (137.2 × 152.4 × 116.8 cm)

Page 375: Marcel Broodthaers, *Ovale d'oeufs 1234567 (Oval
of eggs 1234567)*, 1965. Eggshells and oil paint on wood
panel. 39⅜ × 31½ × 4¾ in. (100 × 80 × 12.1 cm)

Page 376: Naksuyuki Nakanishi, *Ningen no Chizu (Map of
Human)*, 1959. Paint, enamel, and sand on plywood.
48½ × 84¾ in. (123.2 × 215.3 cm)

Page 377: Lee Ufan, *From Point*, 1978. Glue and stone pigment
on canvas. 71½ × 89⅜ in. (181.6 × 227 cm)

Page 378: Gabriel Orozco, *Inner Circles of the Wall*, 1999.
Plaster and graphite. Installation width: approximately 35 ft.
(10.7 m)

Page 379: Mimmo Rotella, *Senza titolo (Untitled)*, 1954.
Back of poster. 23⅝ × 21⅝ in. (60 × 54.9 cm)

Page 380: Alighiero Boetti, *Zig Zag*, 1996. Fabric and aluminum.
19⅝ × 19⅝ × 19⅝ in. (49.8 × 49.8 × 49.8 cm)

Pages 24–29, 56–61, 84–93, 112–17, 136–45, 176–81,
204–209, 228–37, 272–77, 300–309, 344–49: Installation
views of *Geometries On and Off the Grid: Art from 1950
to the Present* at The Warehouse, Dallas, February 2–
November 30, 2015

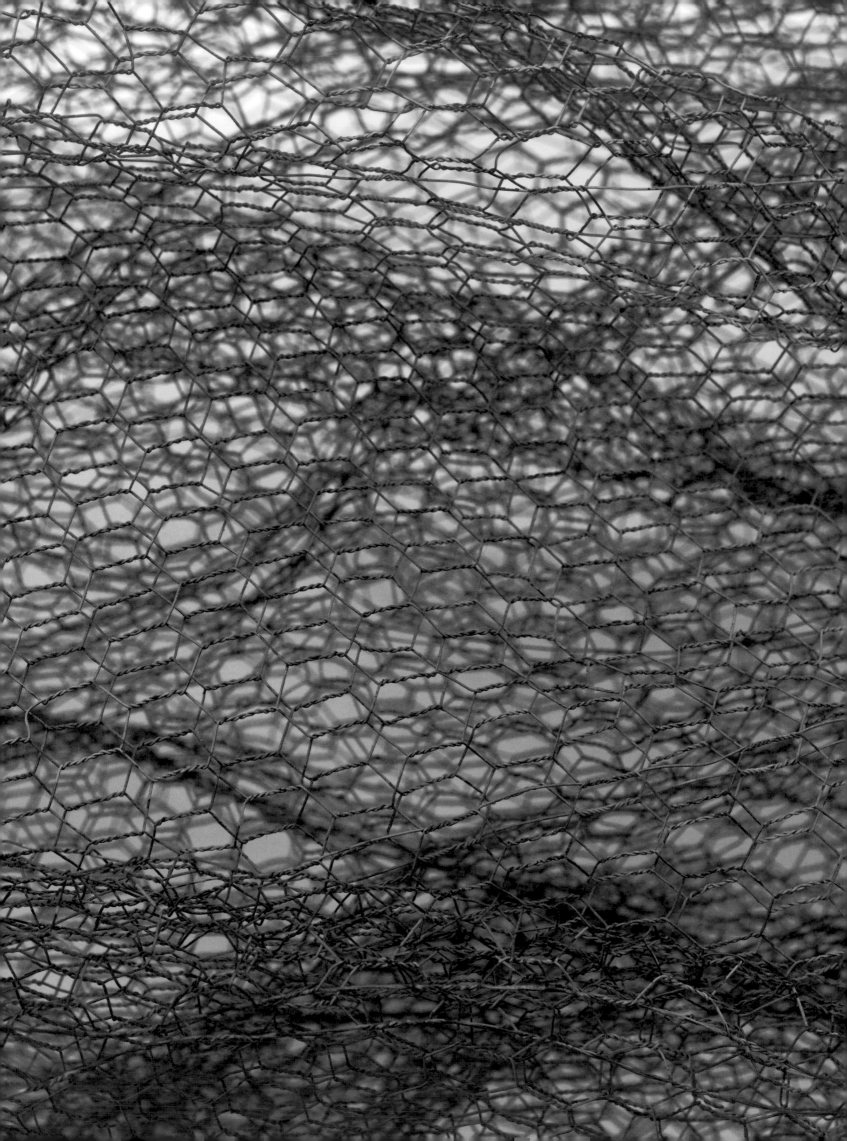

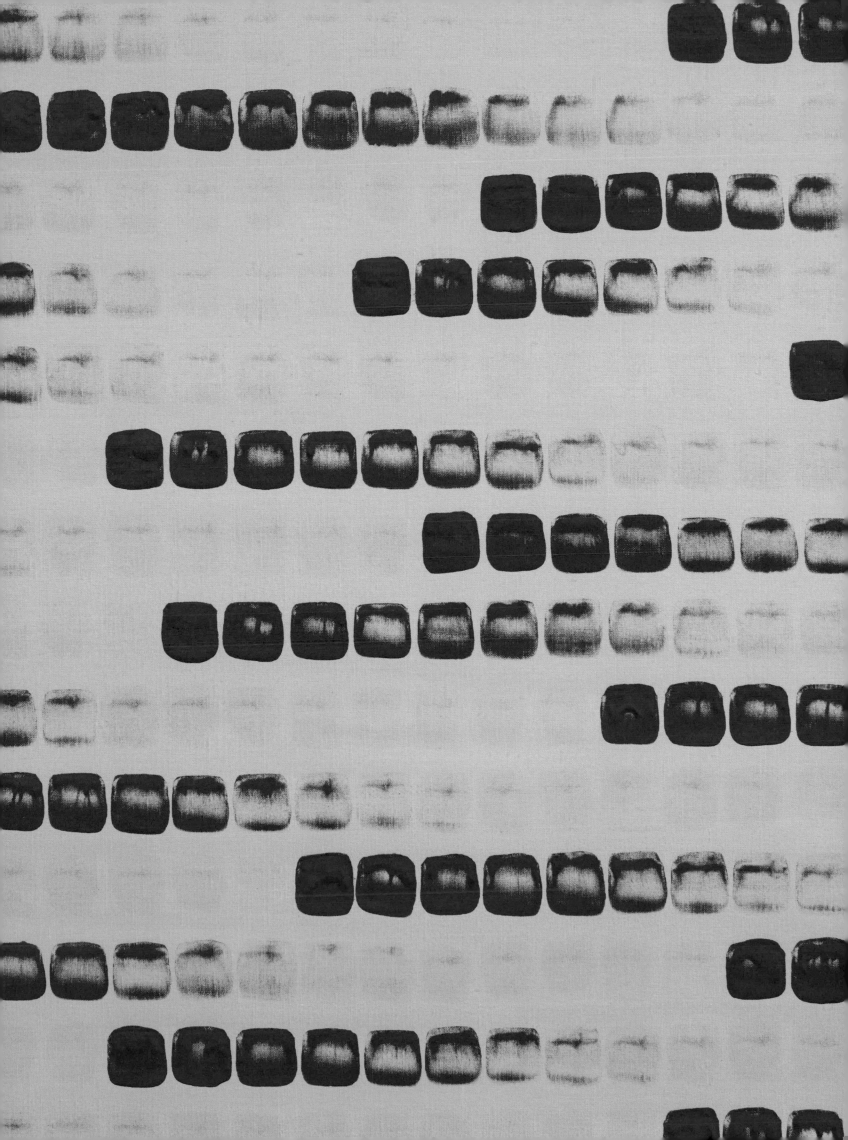